AP® MICROECONOMICS
CRASH COURSE®

By David Mayer, M.Ed.

Research & Education Association
www.rea.com

Research & Education Association
258 Prospect Plains Road
Cranbury, New Jersey 08512
Email: info@rea.com

AP® MICROECONOMICS CRASH COURSE®, 2nd Edition

Printed in the United States of America

Library of Congress Control Number 2019946653

ISBN-13: 978-0-7386-1260-7
ISBN-10: 0-7386-1260-X

AP® MICROECONOMICS CRASH COURSE TABLE OF CONTENTS

PART I

INTRODUCTION

PART II

CONTENT REVIEW

UNIT 1 | BASIC ECONOMIC CONCEPTS

UNIT 2 | SUPPLY AND DEMAND

UNIT 3 | PRODUCTION, COST, AND THE PERFECT COMPETITION MODEL

ABOUT OUR BOOK

REA's *AP® Microeconomics Crash Course* is designed for the last-minute studier or any student who wants a quick refresher on the AP® course. This *Crash Course* is based on the latest changes to the AP® Microeconomics course and exam and focuses only on the topics tested, so you can make the most of your study time.

Written by a veteran AP® Microeconomics test expert, our *Crash Course* gives you a concise review of the major concepts and important topics tested on the AP® Microeconomics exam.

Part I gives you score-raising tips so you can tackle the exam with confidence. It also provides a list of **Key Terms** that you absolutely must know.

Part II presents a **Content Review** that covers every critical aspect of today's exam, including basic economic concepts, demand and supply, production and costs, perfect competition, factor markets, and more.

Part III provides an essential summary of the **Key AP® Microeconomics Graphs and Formulas** you'll need to know for the course and the exam.

Part IV gives you specific **Test-Taking Strategies** to conquer the multiple-choice and free-response questions, along with AP®-style practice questions to prepare you for what you'll see on test day.

ABOUT OUR ONLINE PRACTICE EXAM

How ready are you for the AP® Microeconomics exam? Find out by taking **REA's online practice exam** available at *www.rea.com/studycenter*. This test features automatic scoring, detailed explanations of all answers, and diagnostic score reporting that will help you identify your strengths and weaknesses so you'll be ready on exam day!

Whether you use this book throughout the school year or as a refresher in the final weeks before the exam, REA's *Crash Course* will show you how to study efficiently and strategically, so you can boost your score.

Good luck on your AP® Microeconomics exam!

ABOUT OUR AUTHOR

David Mayer is the Academic Dean at John Paul Stevens High School in San Antonio, Texas. Mr. Mayer developed and taught the AP® Economics program at San Antonio's Winston Churchill High School. More than 600 of his students earned college credit based on their exam performance.

In addition to his work in the classroom, Mr. Mayer serves as an AP® Economics consultant for the College Board and has served as an AP® Economics Reader and Table Leader. He has also written several economics books and test preps.

Mr. Mayer earned his B.S. in Economics from Texas A&M University and his M.Ed. in Educational Psychology from the University of Texas at San Antonio.

ABOUT REA

Founded in 1959, Research & Education Association (REA) is dedicated to publishing the finest and most effective educational materials—including study guides and test preps—for students of all ages.

Today, REA's wide-ranging catalog is a leading resource for students, teachers, and other professionals. Visit *www.rea.com* to see a complete listing of all our titles.

ACKNOWLEDGMENTS

We would like to thank Larry B. Kling, Editorial Director, for his overall guidance; Pam Weston, Publisher, for setting the quality standards for production integrity and managing the publication to completion; John Paul Cording, Technology Director, for managing the REA Study Center; and Jennifer Calhoun for file prep.

We would also like to extend our appreciation to Jason Welker for technically reviewing the manuscript; and Kathy Caratozzolo of Caragraphics for typesetting this edition.

PART I

INTRODUCTION

PART I

INTRODUCTION

How to Score Well
on the AP® Microeconomics Exam

So either you are thinking about or have already signed up to take the AP® Microeconomics exam. Maybe you never took the course, or, heaven forbid, you slept through it. If so, it sounds like what you need is a crash course in microeconomics. Fortunately, you have come upon a book that will give you exactly what you need to score a 4 or 5 on the exam. This book is not meant to be a detailed study of microeconomics, but is instead a straight-to-the-point guide for ensuring your success on the AP® Microeconomics exam.

Know the Structure of the Exam

Students from around the globe sign up to take the AP® Microeconomics exam during the second week in May every year. They come from thousands of schools and represent a variety of cultures, languages, and economic backgrounds. One thing they have in common is that they all are competing with you for college credit in microeconomics. It is true that you have some competition, but do not fret. After studying this *Crash Course* guide you will be more than prepared to score a 5 on the AP® Microeconomics exam!

The AP® Microeconomics exam is made up of two sections. The first is the multiple-choice section, which is comprised of 60 multiple-choice questions. Students have 70 minutes to take the multiple-choice section, meaning that you have a little more than a minute to answer each question. Afterward, students are given the free-response questions and have 10 minutes to read the questions and plan their responses. Once the 10-minute planning period ends, students have 50 minutes to answer the three questions. The first question is the longest and is worth 10 of the 20 points on the free-response section. The next two questions are shorter, equally weighted, and are worth 5 points each. When all is said and done, a total of 90 points is possible on the AP® Microeconomics exam— 60 points from the multiple-choice section and a weight-adjusted 30 from the free-response section.

The multiple-choice section of the exam is scored by machine. Scores on the multiple-choice section are based only on the number of questions answered correctly. Points are not deducted for incorrect answers and no points are awarded for unanswered questions. If you do not know the answer, try to eliminate as many choices as you can and then select the best answer from the remaining choices.

The three free-response questions are scored by AP® readers in early June. Readers include college professors and experienced AP® economics teachers, who meet for this purpose. Every effort is made to ensure objectivity and fairness in assessing each answer to the free-response questions.

Unlike tests given in the classroom which measure the percentage of the material you know, the AP® exams are scored to reveal how much you know relative to everyone else taking the exam. As long as you know more than most other test-takers, you should do just fine. The following table is a sample of how the scores out of 90 points in a given year might translate to results. It should give you a better understanding of how to judge your results on sample exams or set your own specific goal.

Score Range	AP® Grade	Minimum Percent Right
72–90	5	80%
54–71	4	60%
45–53	3	50%
30–44	2	33%
0–27	1	0%

This table is not a misprint! As you can see, scoring 80% will get you a 5, 60% a 4, and 50% a 3. Each year these cutoff scores vary slightly (for example, rather than 72 points needed for a 5, some years 70 points is enough and other years 75 might be needed). Obviously, this test is very different from what you usually see in the classroom.

Know the College Board's Course Outline

The AP® Microeconomics exam is based on the College Board's latest Course and Exam Description. This course framework shows what topics are on the exam. It also shows what percentage of the multiple-choice section of the exam is devoted to the different topics in microeconomics.

Topic	Percentage of Multiple-Choice Questions	Number of Questions Out of 60
Unit 1: Basic Economic Concepts	12%–15%	7–9
Unit 2: Supply and Demand	20%–25%	12–15
Unit 3: Production, Cost, and the Perfect Competition Model	22%–25%	13–15
Unit 4: Imperfect Competition	15%–22%	9–13
Unit 5: Factor Markets	10%–13%	6–8
Unit 6: Market Failure and the Role of Government	8%–13%	5–8

Know When to Guess in the Multiple-Choice Section

Students often wonder, "If I have no idea which of the five options is correct, should I guess?" Since there is no penalty for wrong answers, guessing is always advised if, of course, you have no idea of the correct answer. Before resorting to a blind guess, you should use all your knowledge and understanding of economics to eliminate the possible incorrect answers, so that any guess you are forced to make is an *educated guess.*

Know the Importance of Diagrams

To earn a 4 or 5 on the AP® Micro exam, you must possess more that just a solid understanding of the course material. You also must be skilled at illustrating the concepts from the course in detailed, correctly drawn economics diagrams.

The good news is, all the graphs you need to know are drawn exactly as they should be drawn on the exam right here in this *Crash Course*. Study these diagrams closely as you progress through the book. Examine the labels, the shapes of the lines, the way arrows are used to indicate directions of shifts, and the way dotted lines are used to identify equilibrium points on the axes. Seek to understand the meaning of the various microeconomics models in this book, not just memorize them.

Drawing graphs well (and being able to interpret their meaning in the multiple-choice section) is a crucial skill that will certainly impress the examiners who read your free-response answers. Each line on a graph should be seen as telling a story—a relationship between the variables on the axes of that particular graph. If you strive for understanding why each line is shaped as it is, of what it is composed, and which factors can shift it, you will perform well on graph-based questions whether you encounter them in the multiple-choice or free-response section of the test.

Using College Board Materials to Supplement Your *Crash Course*

This *Crash Course* contains everything you need to know to succeed on the exam. You should, however, supplement it with other materials designed specifically for studying AP® Microeconomics. Visit the College Board's AP® Central website for the full text of the *AP® Microeconomics Course and Exam Description* and sample questions.

Know This Book!

This book has been written so that you will be successful on the AP® Microeconomics exam. The book is divided into the following sections.

Chapter 2 includes all of the key vocabulary that you should know prior to taking the exam.

Chapters 3 through 11 are a concise breakdown of the entire AP® Microeconomics course outline with emphasis on those areas most often tested.

Chapter 12 includes all of the graphs that you must know and might have to draw.

Chapter 13 includes the formulas you are expected to know. According to the College Board, 20% to 30% of the multiple-choice questions on the exam will include analyzing numbers or performing calculations.

Finally, Chapters 14 through 16 provide you with test-taking strategies for both the multiple-choice and free-response sections, along with AP®-style practice questions to prepare you for test day.

With this book and a little work, you should achieve a score of 5 on the AP® Microeconomics exam.

Let's get started!!!

Key Terms

Unit 1: Basic Economic Concepts

1. Absolute Advantage

The ability to produce more of a good or service than another person or society with the same number of inputs. Alternatively, it means one person or society can make a unit of output with fewer units of input than its counterpart.

2. Allocative Efficiency

The amount of production that benefits society the most. It is achieved when the marginal benefit of production equals the marginal cost. Also known as the socially optimal level of output. A society is *allocatively efficient* when it is choosing to make the mix of goods that best satisfy the wants of its population.

3. Capital

The tools, machines, factories, and buildings used to produce goods and services. Includes physical capital, which ranges from hammers to industrial robots and human capital, which is "know-how" or specialized skills that get fused to labor through education and training.

4. Ceteris Paribus

"Other things being equal." The assumption that all variables remain constant except for those being studied by the economist. *Ceteris paribus* allows economists to understand the relationship between economic variables. As in science, economists like to try to isolate one factor that may be changing at a given time to better understand cause and effect.

5. Circular Flow

A model or diagram showing how households and firms interact in product and resource markets. *Circular flow* models help visualize how expenditures become income and how market types relate to one another. Complex versions of the *circular flow* can include activities of government in regulating or participating in various markets and/or international trade.

6. Command Economy

An economic system in which government planners make most of the choices for the economy and answer the basic questions of what to produce, how to produce, and for whom to produce. Often contrasted with *market economy* because these are the two basic extremes; societies can choose strategies for managing the scarcity problem that place them along the spectrum between these two extremes.

7. Comparative Advantage

The ability to produce a good or service at a lower opportunity cost than someone else. Having *comparative advantage* in production of a good is the basis of the economic argument for why specialization and trade can benefit two individuals or societies.

8. Economics

The study of the choices that presumptively rational people make to get what they need and want, given the condition of scarcity. This field of inquiry is divided into macroeconomics—which concerns itself with how societies manage scarcity—and microeconomics—which primarily focuses on how firms and households make choices based on incentives to achieve their objectives.

9. Economist

An individual who studies economics.

10. **Entrepreneur**

    An individual who possesses the factor of production called entrepreneurship. *Entrepreneurs* run firms that attempt to maximize profit.

11. **Entrepreneurship**

    The special ability of some individuals to take risks and combine land, labor, and capital in new ways in order to make profits by providing a good or service instead of selling their labor to an employer.

12. **Factors of Production**

    The resources used to produce goods and services. These include land, labor, capital, and entrepreneurship.

13. **Labor**

    People's mental and/or physical effort and skill used in producing goods and services.

14. **Land**

    Natural resources used in producing goods and services. An economist's definition of land includes land area and the minerals, oil, timber, and other useful bounty that the land provides. Sometimes it is even used so broadly as to be nearly synonymous with *raw materials.*

15. **Law of Increasing Opportunity**

    As the production of one good increases, producers must sacrifice ever-increasing amounts of the other goods because factors of production are not perfectly interchangeable between the production of both goods.

16. **Marginal Benefit**

    The additional benefit of consuming one extra unit of a good or service. The rate of change or slope of total benefit.

17. **Marginal Cost**

    The additional cost of producing one extra unit of a good or service. The rate of change or slope of total cost.

18. **Market**

   A forum for interactions between demanders wishing to make purchases and suppliers wishing to make sales. Markets exist wherever buyers and sellers meet to exchange goods, services, or the factors of production.

19. **Market Economy**

   An economic system that relies on individuals pursuing their own self-interest in the market in order to cope with scarcity. In market systems, prices are used to guide production decisions in a decentralized manner. Buyers "vote" with their spending dollars, making those goods more expensive, thereby encouraging producers to make more of goods that are more desired and useful. Contrasted with *command economy* in which production decisions are made centrally.

20. **Opportunity Cost**

   That which is given up when a choice is made about the use of a scarce resource. *Opportunity cost* includes explicit costs (money payments made) and implicit costs (nonmonetary costs or sacrifices)

21. **Production Possibilities Curve**

   An economic model that shows all of the possible combinations of two goods that could be produced using scarce factors of production.

22. **Production Possibilities Frontier**

   See *Production Possibilities Curve.*

23. **Productive Efficiency**

   The condition that exists when the least amount of waste happens in producing as much output as possible. When a society is using all its resources to produce goods and services, it is *productively efficient.*

24. **Scarcity**

   The fundamental problem of economics. The condition that exists because people's wants and needs are greater than the available resources to meet those wants and needs.

25. Specialization

A person or society's decision to focus production on a particular good or service, leading it to trade with others for the remaining goods it needs. To achieve maximum benefit, the person or society should specialize according to their comparative advantage.

26. Terms of Trade

The rate at which people trade two goods. The ratio or "real price" for which a unit of one good can be purchased for units of another good.

27. Trade-Off

An alternative use for scarce factors of production. *Trade-offs* are a result of scarcity and inherently connected to the making of choices.

II. Unit 2: Supply and Demand

1. Complementary Goods

Goods that are consumed together, such as cars and gasoline or peanut butter and jelly.

2. Consumer(s)

People who buy goods and services. Often a household is considered to be a fundamental unit of consumption.

3. Consumer Surplus

The difference between the equilibrium price in the market and the price consumers are actually willing to pay for a good or service. On a graph, *consumer surplus* is represented as the area beneath the demand curve, above the price paid, and to the left of the quantity purchased.

4. Cross-Price Elasticity

The percentage change in the quantity demanded for one good divided by the percentage change in the price of a related good. *Cross-price elasticity* determines whether goods are complements (if negative) or substitutes (if positive).

5. Deadweight Loss

The loss of consumer and producer surplus that occurs when a quantity other than the equilibrium quantity prevails in the market. *Deadweight loss* results from over- or under-production of a good and is associated with *allocative inefficiency.*

6. Demand

The willingness and ability of consumers to buy goods and services at the various prices that exist in the market within a specified time frame. Describes the inverse relationship between the quantity demanded and the price that is often expressed as a graphical curve or a tabular schedule.

7. Demand Curve

A downward-sloping curve that illustrates consumers' demand for goods and services at various prices.

8. Determinants of Demand

The factors that cause demand to either increase or decrease. The *determinants of demand* include: market size, expected prices, related prices, income, and consumer tastes.

9. Determinants of Supply

The factors that cause supply to either increase or decrease. The *determinants of supply* include: technology, related prices, input prices, competition, government taxes and subsidies, and expected prices.

10. Diminishing Marginal Utility

Each additional unit of a good or service that is consumed gives less additional satisfaction or utility than the previous unit that was consumed. One of the reasons why price and quantity demanded have an inverse relationship.

11. Effective Price Ceiling

A price ceiling is a legal maximum price set below the equilibrium price. This results in the quantity demanded exceeding the quantity supplied at the ceiling price. Hence a shortage exists in the market.

12. Effective Price Floor

A *price floor* is a legal minimum price set above the equilibrium price. This results in the quantity supplied exceeding the quantity demanded at the floor price. Hence a surplus exists in the market.

13. Elasticity

The sensitivity of quantity changes relative to changes in other factors, often prices.

14. Elastic

Describes a rate of change in quantity that is greater (in percentage terms) than the rate of change in price.

15. Equilibrium

The condition that exists in the market when a single price and quantity result from the intersection of supply and demand. The natural price-quantity combination at which neither a shortage nor a surplus exists.

16. Excise Tax

A per-unit tax on the production of a good or service. *Excise taxes* tend to reduce supply, decreasing quantity of a good that is sold and increasing the price that buyers pay.

17. Income Effect

Consumers' buying power changes inversely to changes in price. This is one reason for the inverse relationship expressed in the *law of demand*. Consumers buy fewer units at higher prices because their same nominal income has less purchasing power.

18. Income Elasticity of Demand

The percentage change in the quantity demanded divided by the percentage change in consumers' income. Measures whether and how much buying increases (typically) or decreases (unusual in cases of less-desirable goods) when income rises. *Income elasticity of demand* determines whether goods are normal (if positive) or inferior (if negative).

19. Inelastic

Describes a rate of change in quantity that is less (in percentage terms) than the rate of change in price.

20. Inferior Good

A good whose demand varies inversely with consumers' incomes.

21. Law of Demand

The price and quantity demanded of a good are inversely related because of income effect, substitution effect, and diminishing marginal benefits.

22. Law of Increasing Marginal Cost

The cost of producing each additional unit of a good or service incurs a greater cost than the previous unit. Results from the need to use resources that are less and less well-suited to production of that good as quantity produced increases.

23. Law of Supply

The price and quantity supplied of a good are directly related. Higher prices induce increased production quantities.

24. Marginal Utility

The additional satisfaction or usefulness a consumer gets from consuming an additional unit of a good or service. Change in total utility divided by change in quantity consumed.

25. Normal Good

A good whose demand varies directly with consumers' incomes.

26. Price Ceiling

A maximum price for a good or service that cannot be legally exceeded. See *Effective Price Ceiling*.

27. **Price Elasticity of Demand**

The responsiveness of quantity changes relative to price changes; the percentage change of quantity demanded divided by the percentage change in price.

28. **Price Elasticity of Supply**

The percentage change in quantity supplied divided by the percentage change in the price of a good or service.

29. **Price Floor**

A minimum price for a good or service that cannot be legally undermined. See *Effective Price Floor*.

30. **Producer(s)**

People who make and sell goods and services; suppliers.

31. **Producer Surplus**

The difference between the market equilibrium price and the price producers would willingly accept for a good or service. On a graph, *producer surplus* is represented by the area beneath the price received, above the supply (or marginal cost) curve, and to the left of quantity sold.

32. **Quantity Demanded**

The amount of a good or service that consumers are willing and able to buy at a given price in a specified period of time.

33. **Quantity Supplied**

The amount of a good or service that producers are willing and able to sell at a given price in a specified period of time.

34. **Shortage**

The condition that exists when the quantity demanded exceeds the quantity supplied. Indication of price being lower than equilibrium level.

35. **Substitute Goods**

Goods which are used in place of each other. For example, margarine is a substitute for butter.

36. Substitution Effect

The tendency of consumers to substitute lower-priced items for higher-priced items. A reason why the *law of demand* is true; consumers purchase fewer units at higher prices because substitutes (whose prices are unchanged) seem relatively cheaper.

37. Supply

The willingness and ability of producers to offer a good or service for sale at the various prices which exist in the market within a certain time frame. The positive or direct relationship between quantity supplied and price that is often displayed on a graphical curve or in a tabular schedule.

38. Supply Curve

An upward-sloping curve that illustrates producers' willingness and ability to bring units of a good or service to market during a particular time period.

39. Surplus

The condition that exists when the quantity supplied exceeds the quantity demanded. Indication of price being higher than equilibrium level.

40. Total Revenue

The price of a good or service multiplied by the quantity sold. Total receipts a firm takes in from selling its finished goods and services.

41. Total Revenue Test

A test for *price elasticity of demand*. If price changes vary directly with total revenue, then the demand is inelastic. If price changes vary inversely with total revenue, then the demand is elastic. If price changes do not cause a change in total revenue, then demand is *unit elastic.*

42. Unit Elastic

Describes percentage change in quantity that is equal to percentage change in price.

43. Utility

The want-satisfying power that goods and services provide. The amount of usefulness or satisfaction that a consumer gets from consuming a good or service.

44. Utility Maximization

Economists assume that consumers always try to maximize their total utility. With a budget, consumers seek combinations of the goods they buy which yield the greatest overall level of satisfaction.

45. Utility Maximization Rule

A formula that illustrates the combination of two goods that maximize a consumer's utility. The formula is $\dfrac{MUx}{Px} = \dfrac{MUy}{Py}$.

Can be extended to any number of goods and implies that customers do best when they try to ensure that the last dollar they spend on each type of good they purchase yields the same level of added satisfaction.

III. Unit 3: Production, Cost, and the Perfect Competition Model

1. Accounting Profit

Total revenue minus the explicit costs of production. For example, if a firm sells 100 beach balls at $2 per ball, then total revenue equals $200. If the firm spends $125 on labor, capital, and materials, then the accounting profit equals $200 − $125 = $75.

2. Average Fixed Cost (AFC)

Fixed cost divided by the quantity of a firm's output. Decreases at decreasing rate as output rises.

3. Average Total Cost (ATC)

The sum of average fixed cost and average variable cost. Total costs incurred divided by number of units produced. Typically falls and then rises as output increases.

4. Average Variable Cost (AVC)

Variable cost divided by the quantity of a firm's output. Typically falls and then rises as output increases.

5. Average Product

The total product of a firm divided by the amount of a particular input used to produce the total product.

6. Barriers to Entry

Anything that prohibits or discourages new firms from entering into a market. Perfect competition is assumed to have no significant barriers to the entry of new firms or the exit of existing firms from the industry in the long run.

7. Commodity

A good that is identical regardless of which firm produced it.

8. Constant Returns to Scale

This exists when a firm's long-run average total cost remains constant as the firm's size increases.

9. Decreasing (Marginal) Returns

This happens when total product and marginal product both decrease as an input is added to the production process.

10. Diminishing Marginal Returns

This happens when marginal product is decreasing while total product is still increasing as an input is added to the production process.

11. Diseconomy of Scale

This exists when a firm's long-run average total cost increases as the firm's size increases. The firm becomes less productively efficient as output rises in the long run. Also known as *decreasing returns to scale*.

12. Economic Profit

Profits earned by a firm over and above *normal profit*. Areas of profit shown on economics graphs are economic profit (or loss) and encourage new firms to join industries in which they can expect to earn more than normal profit.

To calculate economic profit, you must take the *accounting profit* minus the opportunity cost of production. For example, assume that a firm has an accounting profit of $75. If the firm's resources could have earned an accounting profit of $70 in another industry, then the economic profit equals $75 − $70 = $5.

13. **Economy of Scale**

    This exists when a firm's long-run average total cost declines as the firm's size increases. The firm becomes more productively efficient as output rises in the long run. Also known as *increasing returns to scale*.

14. **Firm**

    An organization that produces a good or service in order to make a profit for its owner or owners. Many people refer to a firm as a business. A fundamental assumption of economics is that firms seek to maximize profit.

15. **Fixed Cost**

    A cost that does not change as a firm's production changes. *Fixed costs* are incurred prior to producing even the first unit.

16. **Homogenous Products**

    Products that are identical or so similar that consumers can't or don't distinguish between the products made by various firms. Perfectly competitive industries are assumed to feature many firms producing goods that cannot be distinguished from one another and therefore are perfectly substitutable for one another.

17. **Increasing (Marginal) Returns**

    This happens when both total and marginal product increase as an input is added to the production process.

18. **Long Run**

    The production period in which all of a firm's inputs can be varied and in which firms can enter or exit various industries.

19. Long-Run Average Total Cost (LRATC)

A graph which shows a firm's average total cost as it varies its size and displays economies of scale (if downward sloping) and/or diseconomies of scale.

20. Marginal Cost (MC)

The cost of producing an additional unit of output. Change in total cost divided by change in output.

21. Marginal Product

The additional output which is produced when an additional unit of input, often labor, is added to the production process.

22. Normal Profit

Amount of accounting profit that a firm would earn equal to fair market value of the resources the firm's owner uses. In particular, this includes the wages or salary that the entrepreneur could have earned working for another firm. *Normal profit* exists when a firm earns zero economic profit in an industry. *Normal profit* provides neither an incentive for firms to enter or exit the industry.

23. Perfect Competition

A market condition in which buyers and sellers have no influence over price because they are small, independent, trade in commodities, and are unable to place barriers to entry or exit from the market.

24. Price Taker

Firms in perfect competition are assumed to be *price takers* because they cannot control the market price for the good they sell. Due to the number of sellers of homogenous goods, each seller can sell any quantity it wants at the market price. Above this price, they would sell zero units. This means they face demand curves which are horizontal or perfectly elastic.

25. Production Function

The amount of output varies as inputs are added in production. Typically, output increases as inputs are added, but often at a decreasing rate.

26. Profit

The *revenue* a firm has remaining after paying all of its costs. See *Economic, Normal,* and *Accounting Profit.*

27. Short Run

The period of production time in which at least one input is constant.

28. Total Cost

The sum of fixed and variable costs. Economists include implicit costs (normal profits) as costs.

29. Total Product

All of a firm's output created by its inputs; synonym for *quantity produced.*

30. Variable Cost

A cost that changes with the firm's level of production.

IV. Unit 4: Imperfect Competition—Monopoly

1. Copyright

The government protection of someone's intellectual property from being taken or sold by another. Serves as a barrier to entry of new firms, giving the owner of the copyright monopoly power.

2. Geographic Monopoly

A market condition in which a firm faces no competition in a certain geographic area.

3. Government Monopoly

A market condition in which government provides a good or service and prevents the private sector from competing in the market. Related to the idea of public goods.

4. Natural Monopoly

A market condition in which a firm is able to prevent competition because its *economy of scale* allows it to produce at a lower average total cost than any smaller competitor could.

5. Patent

A government-granted license to be the sole producer of a new good or service. Similar in function to a copyright because it is a source of monopoly power for the sole legal producer.

6. Perfect Price Discrimination

The ability of a monopolist to charge each individual consumer the highest price the consumer would willingly pay for a good or service. Because each buyer pays his or her reservation price, there is no consumer surplus if a firm *perfectly price discriminates*.

7. Price Discrimination

The ability of some producers to charge consumers different prices for the same good or service. When firms *price discriminate*, they sell some units at high prices and other units at lower prices, usually on the basis of different customers' willingness to pay.

8. Technological Monopoly

A market condition in which the firm's possession of either a patent or copyright prevents other firms from legally competing in the market for a good or service.

V. Unit 4: Imperfect Competition—Monopolistic Competition

1. Excess Capacity

The difference in the long run between the quantity that a perfectly competitive market produces and the quantity produced by monopolistically competitive firms. Underutilization of the factories or productive capabilities of each firm; amount by which a firm would increase production in order to be productively efficient.

2. Monopolistic Competition

A relatively competitive market structure in which many firms compete, each having a limited ability to set prices and earn economic profits because of product differentiation.

3. Product Differentiation

The efforts by firms to make their products appear different from those of their competitors. Also known as non-price competition, this involves firms making all sorts of claims about the relative quality of their product or service. Location, reliability, friendly employees, community tradition, social responsibility, popularity with the masses, and an air of exclusivity related to the product are all types of claims firms make to differentiate their products.

VI. Unit 4: Imperfect Competition—Oligopoly and Game Theory

1. Cartel

A group of producers in an industry who collude in order to form a functional monopoly. *Cartels* are illegal in many countries and tend to be rare and unstable due to the incentives their member firms often have to cheat on agreed prices and/or quantities.

2. Collusion

Agreement by producers in an industry to cooperate and set prices instead of competing with one another. Considered an unethical or illegal practice, *collusion* makes *oligopolies* function more like *monopolies*.

3. **Dominant Strategy**

   In game theory, a strategy in which a player always chooses independent of the other player's choice. For a choice to be a *dominant strategy*, it must be the best response a player could choose from all of the choices available to the other player.

4. **Game Theory**

   The study of strategic decision-making used in economics and many other disciplines in which analysis of interdependent choices is performed. To an economist, a *game* is a situation in which a discrete number of players can be identified, each has specific strategies or choices, and the payoffs to each player can be quantified (or approximated) for strategic analysis.

5. **Interdependence**

   The condition in which the decisions of producers are based on the possible decisions of other producers. Oligopolies feature *interdependence* because firms must take into consideration the actions of other firms when determining their optimal price and quantity.

6. **Nash Equilibrium**

   In game theory, it is the condition where a player has no incentive to change their strategy after considering the other player's choices. It is possible to have no, one, or multiple Nash equilibria in a payoff matrix.

7. **Oligopoly**

   A market structure in which a few firms dominate and behave interdependently. Entry of new firms is often quite difficult, usually because of the size of existing firms.

8. **Payoff Matrix**

   A grid that shows the outcomes of decisions made by producers in a game. Based on a payoff matrix, dominant strategies can be determined.

9. Price Leadership Model

Type of *oligopoly* in which one firm functionally sets the price for the industry. Other firms either defer to the price leader due to its size or traditional role as the anchor firm in the industry.

10. Prisoner's Dilemma

An equilibrium in a game where the dominant strategy for each player results in an outcome where neither player maximizes their total utility.

VII. Unit 5: Factor Markets

1. Derived Demand

Demand for goods and services creates a demand for the factors of production to produce those goods and services. Thus, demand for resources is derived from (and changes with) the demand for the products those resources make.

2. Factor Market

The market in which the factors of production are bought by firms and sold by households.

3. Marginal Factor Cost

The cost of employing one additional unit of a factor; change in total cost divided by change in quantity of the factor in question (often labor). Bears a close relationship to labor supply.

4. Marginal Revenue Product

The added revenue a firm gains when employing an additional unit of a factor. Change in total revenue divided by change in the quantity of the factor in question (often labor). Bears a close relationship to labor demand.

5. Monopsony

A market dominated by a single consumer. The *monopsony* model is used to show why in labor markets with only one large firm hiring all the labor in an area, wages and employment will be lower than if there were several firms bidding for labor resources. *Monopsonies* often give rise to union formation.

6. Wage

The price of labor per unit of time.

7. Wage Taker

Firms who hire labor in perfectly competitive labor markets are wage takers; they can hire any quantity of workers desired for a market wage rate. This stems from the fact that in these markets there are a large number of firms hiring similarly qualified workers. Thus, these firms face horizontal (perfectly elastic) labor supply curves.

8. Unions

Organizations of workers who seek to increase the wage rates, improve working conditions, and expand the number of jobs available in their industries. Unions can be of various types and may seek to include all workers in a sector or make membership more exclusive in a particular craft.

VIII. Unit 6: Market Failure and the Role of Government

1. Estate Tax

A tax assessed on the total value of a person's private property after he/she dies; often assessed only on large estates.

2. Externality

Either a positive or negative side-effect of production and/or consumption. Costs incurred by those who do not produce the product and benefits that accrue to those who are not the purchasers are both examples of *externalities*.

3. Gift Tax

A tax placed on gifts received from another person.

4. **Gini Coefficient**

   The ratio of the area above the Lorenz curve to the total area below the line of equality. *Gini coefficients* range between zero and one. Societies with higher *Gini coefficients* have more unequally distributed wealth or income.

5. **Lorenz Curve**

   A graph that shows the relative equality of the income or wealth distribution in a society.

6. **Marginal Private Benefit**

   The private benefit of consuming an additional unit of a good or service; benefit obtained by the consumer only.

7. **Marginal Private Cost**

   The private cost of producing an additional unit of output; costs incurred by the producer/seller only.

8. **Marginal Social Benefit**

   The benefit to society of consuming an additional unit of a good or service. This includes marginal private benefit and the external benefits that are captured by non-buyers.

9. **Marginal Social Cost**

   The cost to society of producing an additional unit of output. This includes marginal private costs and those external costs that are incurred by third parties.

10. **Market Failure**

    The failure of a market to provide a good/service or to allocate goods/services in a socially optimal manner. Market failure may result from inadequate competition, from externalities, from informational advantages on the part of the buyer or seller, or from other causes.

11. **Negative Externality**

    A side-effect of production or consumption which places a cost on someone other than the consumer or producer of the good or service. These unpaid costs to society lead goods of this type to be overproduced in unregulated markets.

12. Non-Excludable

The condition in which the benefit of a good or service cannot be withheld if a consumer does not pay for it. Non-excludability often leads to the *free rider problem* in which people who would otherwise buy a good choose not to and end up receiving most or all of the benefit anyway.

13. Non-Rival

The condition in which one person's consumption of a good or service does not prevent another person from consuming the exact same good or service. Also known as *shared consumption*.

14. Positive Externality

A side effect of production or consumption which provides a benefit to someone other than the consumer or the producer of the good or service. *Positive externalities* tend to result in underproduction of the good or service in question.

15. Progressive Tax

A tax which takes a greater percentage of income from households with high income than households with low income. The United States income tax is set up in a progressive manner because higher-income earners are in higher tax brackets.

16. Proportional Tax

A tax which takes the same percentage of income from all households.

17. Public Good

A good or service that is provided by the government. Goods tend to work best as public goods if they are non-rival and non-excludable. Public goods are financed by tax revenue.

18. Regressive Tax

A tax which takes a greater percentage of income from households with low income than households with high income.

19. **Rival**

    The condition in which one person's consumption of a good or service prevents another person from consuming the exact same unit of the good or service.

20. **Socially Optimal**

    The market condition that is met when the marginal social benefit equals the marginal social cost. Also known as the *allocatively efficient level of output*.

21. **Subsidy**

    A payment from the government that is made to either a consumer or producer of a good/service. Subsidies function like a negative tax: they encourage production and/or consumption of a good by reducing their production cost.

PART II

CONTENT REVIEW

UNIT 1
BASIC ECONOMIC CONCEPTS

Basic Economic Concepts

Topic 1.1: Scarcity

A. Scarcity

1. No matter who they are or where they are, people's wants and needs are *always* greater than the resources available to meet those wants and needs. This condition is called *scarcity*. Simply put, scarcity exists because our unlimited wants are greater than our limited resources.

2. The scarce resources people use to meet their wants and needs are called the *factors of production*. These include land, labor, capital, and entrepreneurship.

    i. The factor of production that includes all natural resources such as water, soil, trees, oil, and animals is referred to as *land*.

    ii. The factor of production that includes people's physical and mental effort and ability is called *labor*.

    iii. The factor of production that includes tools, machines, factories, and buildings is called *capital*.

    iv. *Entrepreneurship* is the special factor of production that results from some individuals' willingness to take risks by putting land, labor, and capital together in new ways to make a good or service. They do this in order to earn more money than they could if they had just sold their labor to an employer. These entrepreneurs are risk-takers in search of profit.

B. Choice

1. Because all the factors of production are scarce, people are forced to make choices about how to use the factors of production available to them.

2. *Economics* is the study of the choices people make in order to satisfy their unlimited wants with scarce factors of production.

3. The various choices people face when using their limited factors of production are called *trade-offs*.

   i. For example, a carpenter can either use a sheet of plywood to make a cabinet or use it as flooring, but the carpenter cannot use the same sheet of plywood for both purposes. Instead, this carpenter faces a trade-off: use the plywood to make a cabinet or use the plywood as flooring.

II. Topic 1.2: Resource Allocation and Economic Systems

A. Three Questions Every Society Must Answer

1. *What do we produce?* Corn or wheat? Tanks or school buses? Biological weapons or medicine?

2. *How do we produce it?* Is it labor intensive or capital intensive?

3. *Who do we produce it for?* The rich or the poor? Individuals or the state?

B. Command Economy

1. A *command economy* is one in which the three questions are answered by government officials who determine what is produced, how it is produced, and for whom it is produced.

   i. Examples of command economies include North Korea, Cuba, and the former Soviet Union.

C. Market Economy

1. In *market economies*, the three questions are answered primarily by individuals.

2. *Markets* are where buyers and sellers come together in order to trade with each other.

3. Market economies rely on people's self-interest to direct the factors of production to their best use because they regard those factors of production as individually owned.

4. In market economies, people are able to own private property and this gives them an incentive to produce goods or services for others so that they will get goods and services in return.

   i. For example, if a person is hungry, this provides another person an opportunity to make themselves better-off by providing the hungry person with a meal. Because this opportunity exists, people have an incentive to grow food to feed more than just themselves.

   ii. Similarly, if a person owns land which he or she is currently not farming, this person has an incentive to rent the land to someone who does actively wish to farm it. The rent this will generate helps the person consume more than he or she otherwise could.

5. The United States, Hong Kong, and New Zealand are examples of economies closest to a market economy.

III. **Topic 1.3: Production Possibilities Curve**

A. The Model

1. A model is a math equation or graph that simplifies reality. *Economists*, the people who study economics, use models to understand or show economic behavior.

2. When economists make models, they look at how two or three things are related. It is important to know that the models they use are made with the *ceteris paribus* assumption. *Ceteris paribus* means that everything else

stays the same except for the few things the economist is studying.

3. One such model is the *production possibilities curve (PPC)*, also called the *production possibilities frontier (PPF)*. The PPC shows all of the possible combinations of two goods that could be produced if the factors of production are used efficiently, that is, with the least amount of waste. The only thing that changes in the model is the production combination. The amount of resources, time, and technology do not change in the model. If these things do change, then the model changes. Remember *ceteris paribus*?

4. Once a production combination choice is made about using scarce factors of production, there is a cost. Something is given up. This is called *opportunity cost*.

    i. In the example of the carpenter (see page 38), a choice needed to be made about how to use a sheet of plywood. The carpenter studied his or her trade-offs and chose to use the plywood as flooring in a house he or she was building. Because the carpenter used the plywood as flooring material, the opportunity cost was the cabinet the carpenter could have built.

B. Understanding the PPC

1. The PPC (Figure 3.1) shows the possible combinations of lemons and oranges that can be grown on a farm using scarce factors of production. Points A, B, C, and D are all on the curved line labeled *PPC*. If the farmer produces at any of these points, then he or she is being efficient in production. In other words, the farmer is being productively efficient. The farmer can't produce more of one good without giving up more of the other good. To an economist, the farmer is fully employing all of the available factors of production assuming that time, technology, and the factors of production remain constant.

    i. At point A, the farmer is producing eight lemons and zero oranges.

    ii. At point B, the farmer is producing six lemons and five oranges.

iii. At point C, the farmer is producing three lemons and seven oranges.

iv. At point D, the farmer is producing zero lemons and eight oranges.

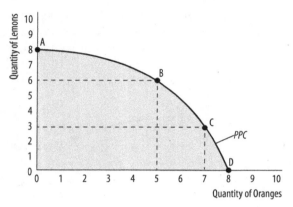

Figure 3.1

2. The PPC above shows trade-offs and opportunity cost. For the farmer, the trade-offs are lemons or oranges.

   i. If the farmer is only producing lemons (point A), then the opportunity cost of producing five oranges will be the two lemons (eight minus six) that he or she must sacrifice in order to produce the first five oranges.

   ii. If the farmer is at point B where he or she produces five oranges, but wants to move to point C and produce seven oranges, then the opportunity cost of producing the next two oranges will be three lemons (six minus three). The opportunity cost of making oranges is rising because the resources available may be better suited to producing lemons. This increasing opportunity cost is what gives the production possibilities curve its concave shape.

3. The PPC in Figure 3.2 is similar to the previous one except that two points, E and F, have been added.

   i. If the farmer is producing at point E (three lemons and five oranges), then this farmer is not being productively efficient. The farmer could produce more of either, without giving up any of the other good.

ii. Can the farmer produce the combination shown by point F (six lemons and seven oranges)? No, the combination lies outside of the farm's production possibilities. To produce six lemons and seven oranges simultaneously, the farmer would need either more factors of production or more technology.

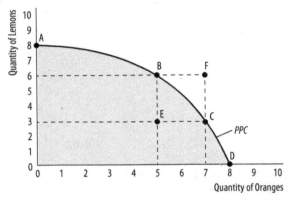

Figure 3.2

4. If there is an increase in the factors of production or technology, then it is possible for the PPC to shift outward as shown in Figure 3.3.

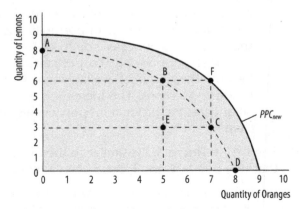

Figure 3.3

5. The PPC illustrated in Figure 3.4 is different than those shown before. Instead of a curve, this PPC is better described as a line. What's the difference? When the PPC is curved, the opportunity cost of producing oranges or lemons increases as production increases. This is called the *law of increasing opportunity cost*. It happens because the factors of production are not perfectly suited for both lemons and oranges.

   i.   For example, some soil, water, and weather conditions are better for oranges and others are better for lemons. In the PPC shown in Figure 3.4 below, the factors of production are perfectly suited for producing either. As a result, the opportunity cost of production stays the same or stays constant.

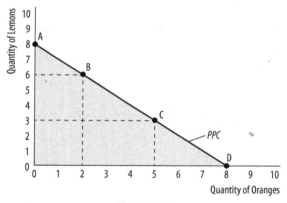

Figure 3.4

Topic 1.4: Comparative Advantage and Trade

A. Why Do People Trade?

1. People trade in order to get what they need or want. Trade happens when people give up one good or service in order to get another good or service. They trade because it makes them better off than if they were self-sufficient.

2. Self-sufficiency exists when you are able to satisfy your needs without trading with anyone.

3. The theory of *comparative advantage* helps to explain why trade makes people better off. *Ceteris paribus* (keeping everything else the same), comparative advantage is the ability to produce a good or service at a lower opportunity cost than that of someone else.

4. *Specialization* happens when people only produce what they have a comparative advantage at producing.

5. *Ceteris paribus, absolute advantage* is the ability to produce more of a good or service than that of someone else. Absolute advantage is *not* an important factor in determining who should produce what, even though at first glance it might seem like it is important.

B. Figuring Out Who Should Produce What

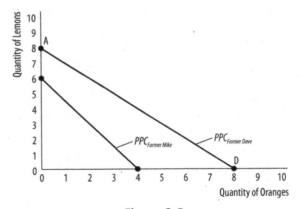

Figure 3.5

1. In the graph above (Figure 3.5), two farmers' PPCs are shown. Farmer Dave can produce eight lemons or eight oranges or any combination shown by his PPC. Farmer Mike can produce six lemons or four oranges or any combination shown by his PPC.

2. Should Farmer Dave trade with Farmer Mike?

   i. At first glance, you might not think so. After all, Farmer Dave can produce more than Farmer Mike. Dave has an absolute advantage in lemons (eight compared to six) and he has an absolute advantage in oranges (eight compared to four).

  ii. Remember that specialization and trade are based upon comparative advantage. To determine comparative advantage you must first calculate the opportunity cost of producing oranges and lemons for Dave and Mike.

> ➤ Dave gives up eight oranges for every eight lemons he produces, which means that every time he produces one lemon he gives up one orange, and when he produces one orange he gives up one lemon.

> ➤ Mike gives up four oranges for every six lemons he produces, which means that every time he produces one lemon he gives up two-thirds of an orange, and when he produces one orange he gives up one and one-half lemons.

> ➤ Based on the opportunity costs above, Dave should specialize in producing oranges because his opportunity cost in oranges is lower (one lemon versus one and one-half lemons). Mike should specialize in lemons because his opportunity cost in lemons is lower (two-thirds of an orange versus one orange).

Test Tip

It helps to draw a table whenever you come across a question that asks you to determine comparative advantage and/or terms of trade. For example, the graph in Figure 3.5 can be simplified into a table (below) that allows you to see absolute advantage, comparative advantage, and mutually beneficial terms of trade.

	Farmer Dave	**Farmer Mike**
Lemons (L)	8 L = 8 O 1 L = 1 O	6 L = 4 O 1 L = $\frac{2}{3}$ O
Oranges (O)	8 O = 8 L 1 O = 1 L	4 O = 6 L 1 O = 1$\frac{1}{2}$ L

iii. Once comparative advantage has been calculated, then all that is left is to figure out *terms of trade*, or the rate at which two people trade. For example, Farmer Dave and Farmer Mike could trade oranges for lemons at a rate of one orange for one and one-third lemons.

iv. The last step is to determine if the terms of trade are mutually beneficial. At a rate of one orange for one and one-third lemons, Dave benefits because he will now get one-third more of a lemon for each orange he gives up. He is better off through trade than he would be being self-sufficient. Why? On his own, Dave only gains one lemon for each orange he gives up. With trade he gains one and one-third lemons for each orange he gives up.

➤ For trade to occur, both people have to benefit. Now consider Farmer Mike. Mike has to give up one and one-half lemons in order to gain an orange when he is being self-sufficient. With trade, he only has to sacrifice one and one-third lemons in order to gain an orange. Mike saves one-sixth of a lemon given these terms of trade. Because both Dave and Mike benefit, the trade is mutually advantageous.

Test Tip

To quickly calculate mutually beneficial terms of trade, look at your table and choose terms of trade that are in between the opportunity costs of production for each person. Look at the table below:

	Farmer Dave	**Farmer Mike**
Lemons (L)	8 L = 8 O 1 L = 1 O	6 L = 4 O $1 L = \frac{2}{3} O$
Oranges (O)	8 O = 8 L 1 O = 1 L	4 O = 6 L $1 O = 1\frac{1}{2} L$

Choosing mutually advantageous terms of trade between the opportunity costs is easy given the table. Look at the second row for lemons. Dave gives up one lemon for one orange, Mike gives up one lemon for two-thirds of an orange. Terms of trade are mutually advantageous if you choose terms of trade such that one lemon is traded for any number of oranges between the range of one and two-thirds. So, terms of trade of one orange for three-fourths of a lemon are mutually advantageous (three-fourths of an orange is in between one orange and two-thirds of an orange).

V. **Topic 1.5: Cost-Benefit Analysis**

A. Marginal Benefit

1. *Marginal benefit* (MB) is the extra benefit gained from consuming an additional good or service.

2. Economists assume that people try to maximize their benefit.

3. Each additional unit of a good or service that people consume gives them less benefit than the previous unit. For example, your first chocolate chip cookie gives you more benefit than your second chocolate chip cookie.

B. Marginal Cost

1. *Marginal cost* (MC) is the extra cost of producing an additional good or service.

2. Economists assume that people try to minimize their cost.

3. Each additional unit of a good or service that people produce costs more than the previous unit because of the law of increasing opportunity cost. For example, people must give up more to produce two woven blankets than to produce one.

C. Allocative Efficiency

1. *Allocative efficiency* happens when the amount of a good or service produced is most beneficial to society. In other words, it is the level of output associated with maximizing society's total benefit.

2. *Allocative efficiency* happens at the point where MB = MC.

3. If MB > MC, then total benefit can be increased by consuming or producing more output.

4. If MB < MC, then total benefit can be increased by consuming or producing less output.

5. The graph below (Figure 3.6) shows *allocative efficiency* at Q.

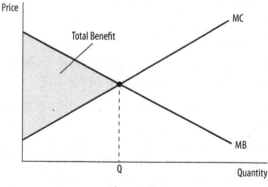

Figure 3.6

VI. **Topic 1.6: Marginal Analysis and Consumer Choice**

A. Utility Maximization

1. Recall that utility is the benefit or satisfaction consumers receive from consuming a good or service.

2. One assumption that economists make about people is that they try to benefit themselves as much as possible or maximize their total satisfaction. Economists call this behavior *utility maximization.*

3. Every time a person consumes an extra unit of a good, they experience *marginal utility*, or extra satisfaction.

4. Marginal utility diminishes as consumption increases.

   i. As an example, consider why it is that people typically order one or two scoops of ice cream versus ordering 49 or 50. After about two scoops most people's satisfaction is probably maxed out. Eventually there comes a point where consumers stop consuming because their added gain of each unit (marginal utility or MU) has fallen to zero. At this point their utility has been maximized (Figure 3.7).

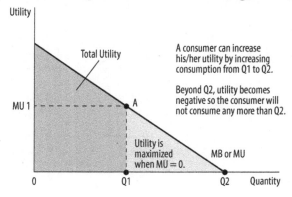

Figure 3.7

5. When consumers have to pay for a good or service at the market-equilibrium price, they will consume up until the point where the marginal utility of their purchase equals the

price of their purchase. The following graphs (Figures 3.8, 3.9, and 3.10) illustrate a consumer's decision to buy more of a good. Utility is maximized at the point where marginal utility (MU) equals price (P).

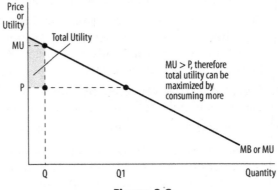

Figure 3.8

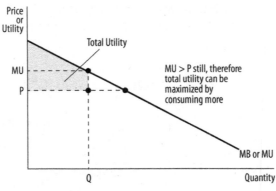

Figure 3.9

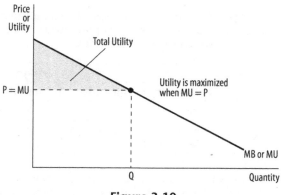

Figure 3.10

B. The Utility-Maximizing Rule

1. How do people decide how much to consume when they are faced with multiple goods and a limited budget? Economists (and you on the AP® exam) use the utility-maximizing rule to illustrate how consumers make this choice.

2. The utility maximizing rule says that a consumer's utility is maximized when the last dollar spent on each of the goods purchased yields the same marginal utility. So, take the marginal utility of good x divided by the price of good x and check to see if it equals the marginal utility of good y divided by the price of good y.

   i. Utility is maximized when MUx / Px = MUy / Py (algebraically equivalent to MUx / MUy = Px / Py).

   ii. For example, a past AP® Microeconomics exam featured the following problem in the free-response section:

(b) The table below shows the quantities, prices, and marginal utilities of two goods, fudge and coffee, which Mandy purchases.

	Fudge	Coffee
Quantity of purchase	10 pounds	7 pounds
Price per pound	$2	$2
Marginal utility of last pound	12	20

Mandy spends all her money and buys only these two goods. In order to maximize her utility, should Mandy purchase more fudge and less coffee, purchase more coffee and less fudge, or maintain her current consumption? Explain.

(c) Assume that consumers always buy 20 units of good R each month regardless of its price.

   (i)   What is the numerical value of the price elasticity of demand for good R?

   (ii) If the government implements a per-unit tax of $2 on good R, how much of the tax will the seller pay?

To solve this free-response question, you would use the Utility Maximizing Rule to determine the correct answer. For Mandy, utility will be maximized when the $\dfrac{\text{MU fudge}}{\text{P fudge}} = \dfrac{\text{MU coffee}}{\text{P coffee}}$ or when $\dfrac{\text{MU fudge}}{\text{MU coffee}} = \dfrac{\text{P fudge}}{\text{P coffee}}$.

Using the second form of the equation (it's easier), you conclude that $\dfrac{12}{20} > \dfrac{\$2}{\$4}$, so if Mandy consumes more fudge and less coffee, then $\dfrac{\text{MU fudge}}{\text{MU coffee}}$ will decrease and the two ratios will balance because as she consumes more fudge, its marginal utility decreases, and as she consumes less coffee its marginal utility increases. As the ratio between these marginal utility values approaches the ratio of the prices of the two goods, total utility will increase until its maximum value when the ratios equate.

Do not spend too much time fretting over the Utility Maximizing Rule. After reviewing hundreds of multiple-choice and free-response questions, there were about two questions that dealt directly with the topic. Know the utility maximizing formula

$$\left(\frac{MUx}{Px} = \frac{MUy}{Py}\right)$$ *and remember that MU diminishes as consumers buy more.*

UNIT 2
SUPPLY AND DEMAND

Topic 2.1: Demand

1. People who buy things are called *consumers*.

2. Consumers' willingness and ability to buy a good or service at the various prices that exist in a market in a given time is called *demand*. Demand expresses an inverse relationship between quantity demanded and price, other things being equal.

3. Consumers tend to buy higher quantities at lower prices than they do at higher prices. This relationship is called the *law of demand*.

4. Three reasons exist for the law of demand:

   i. When the price of a good or service changes, then so does the consumer's ability to purchase the good or service. When prices rise, the consumer's buying power decreases and so the consumer cannot afford to buy as much. When prices fall, the consumer's buying power increases and so the consumer can afford to purchase more. This is referred to as *income effect*.

   ii. When the price of a good changes, it is changing relative to the price of other goods. Consumers tend to substitute away from more expensive goods toward cheaper goods. For example, a person may have a grocery list with both beef and chicken on it. A decrease in the price of chicken will probably lead him or her to purchase more chicken and less beef. An increase in the price of chicken will probably make beef seem relatively cheaper and lead to a lower quantity of chicken purchased. This tendency is referred to as the *substitution effect*.

iii. Each additional unit of a good or service that a person consumes gives them less benefit, usefulness, or *utility* than the previous unit. This is referred to as *diminishing marginal utility*. The decision to consume an additional unit involves the consumer weighing the marginal benefit of the decision against the marginal cost. Because of diminishing marginal utility, the only way a person will consume more of a good is if the marginal cost or price is lower.

Throughout this and other chapters, practice drawing the graphs that are included in the book. Try to do this without looking at the book for help. Check your work and see if everything is EXACTLY like it is in the book. Most free-response questions will test your ability to graph correctly, so it is important that you hone your skills by practicing.

5. Demand can be illustrated using a *demand curve* such as the one below (Figure 4.1).

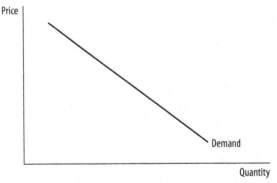

Figure 4.1

i.   In Figure 4.2, point A corresponds to a price of $5 and a quantity demanded of 12.

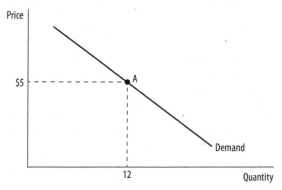

Figure 4.2

ii.   In Figure 4.3, a decrease in the price of a good from $5 to $4 illustrates the law of demand as the quantity demanded increases from 12 to 15. Note that this is a change in quantity demanded and not a change in demand (the function is unchanged, but we have "slid" along it to a different price-quantity combination).

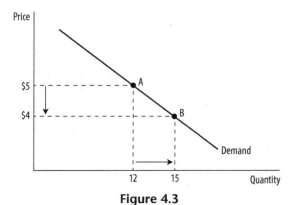

Figure 4.3

II. Topic 2.2: Supply

1. People who make or sell things are called *producers*.

2. Producers' willingness and ability to sell a good or service at the various prices that exist in the market at a given time is called *supply*. Supply expresses a direct or positive relationship between quantity supplied and price, other things being equal.

3. Producers tend to want to offer higher quantities for sale at higher prices than at lower prices. This relationship is called the *law of supply*.

4. The one reason for the law of supply is the *law of increasing marginal cost*. As producers make and sell more, the cost of producing each additional unit increases. This is because of two reasons:

    i. Firms use the cheapest and best-suited resources first and then need to bring factors of production that aren't as useful, easy to obtain, or well-suited to making the good in question. This means that at some point, units become more expensive to make.

    ii. Firms experience *diminishing marginal returns* as they increase production. Even if additional units of labor (for example) are just as well-trained as the first few workers hired, at some point because other factors of production are fixed in the short run (perhaps capital equipment and the factory size), additional workers will increase production by successively less and less.

5. Supply can be illustrated using a *supply curve* such as the one shown in Figure 4.4.

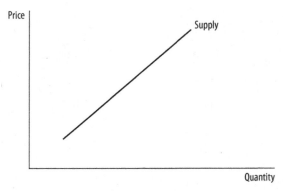

Figure 4.4

i.   In Figure 4.5, point A corresponds to a price of $5 and a quantity supplied of 12.

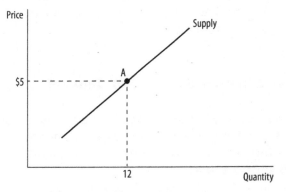

Figure 4.5

ii. In the graph below (Figure 4.6), an increase in the price of a good from $5 to $6 illustrates the law of supply as the quantity supplied increases from 12 to 15.

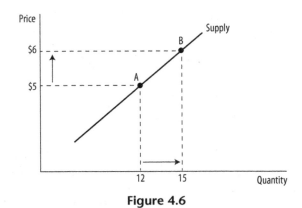

Figure 4.6

     iii. Note that this graph shows an increase in quantity supplied rather than an increase in supply. The supply function is unchanged. A change in price has caused "sliding" along the function to a new price-quantity combination.

III. **Topic 2.3: Price Elasticity of Demand**

    A. In general, *elasticity* measures the sensitivity of quantity changes to price changes. If the quantity change is relatively large compared to the price change, the change can be described as relatively *elastic*.

       1. If the quantity change is proportional to the price change, it can be described as *unit elastic*.

       2. If the quantity change is relatively small compared to the price change, it can be described as *inelastic*.

    B. *Price elasticity of demand* shows the response of quantity demanded to a change in price. Price elasticity is calculated by dividing the rate of change in quantity demanded by the rate of change in price. The formula is

$$Ed = \frac{\% \text{ change in Qd}}{\% \text{ change in P}}$$

for which Ed is price elasticity of demand, Qd is quantity demanded, and P is price.

Interpreting this formula: Since P and Q change in opposite directions (recall the law of demand?), this elasticity coefficient will be negative. Economic convention disregards the negative sign, taking the absolute value, and then comparing it to 1.

1. If Ed < 1, then demand is inelastic.

2. If Ed = 1, then demand is unit elastic.

3. If Ed > 1, then demand is elastic.

C. Another way to determine price elasticity of demand is the *total revenue test*. First, calculate *total revenue* by multiplying price by quantity (P × Q). Compare the change in price to the change in total revenue. If the price and total revenue change in the same direction, then demand is inelastic. If the price changes but total revenue remains constant, then demand is unit elastic. Finally, if price changes, but total revenue moves in the opposite direction, then demand is elastic.

For example, assume tickets to a concert are currently on sale for $100. Organizers estimate they will sell 10,000 tickets at this price for a total revenue ($100 × 10,000 tickets) of $1 million. If they lower the price to $90 and they estimate they will sell $12,000 tickets, is demand elastic, inelastic, or unit elastic? In this case, total revenue would be ($90 × 12,000 tickets) or $1.08 million. Since the price went down and the total revenue increased, then we can conclude that demand for tickets is elastic.

D. The factors that determine price elasticity of demand are whether or not the good is a necessity or a luxury, the availability of substitutes, the amount of time the consumer has available to make a buying decision, and the portion of the consumer's income the purchase would require.

1. If the good or service is a necessity, then demand tends to be inelastic. For example, changes in the price of necessary medicines have little effect on the quantity demanded. To the contrary, a good or service that is not necessary tends to have relatively elastic demand. Luxury goods tend to have

elastic demand, and, unsurprisingly, addictive or habit-form-ing goods tend to have inelastic demand.

2. If no close substitutes exist, demand is inelastic. If ready substitutes are available, demand is elastic. For example, the demand for electricity tends to be inelastic, while the demand for German sports cars is elastic.

3. If ample time to make a decision exists, then demand is elastic. If a purchasing decision must be made immediately, then demand is inelastic. In the short run, gasoline has a very inelastic demand because people are locked into their commuting patterns. Given time, people might be "driven" to use less gas as they first set up carpools, then find alterna-tive modes of transit (by buying hybrid cars or using mass transit), then develop lifestyles that avoid long commutes (by moving closer to work, getting a job closer to home, or telecommuting).

4. A good or service that requires a significant portion of a con-sumer's income to purchase tends to have elastic demand, but a good or service that requires only a small portion of income tends to have inelastic demand. If a $20,000 car increases in price by 10 percent, that $2,000 increase may really change buyers' decisions and reduce sales. But a 100 percent increase in the price of paper clips will probably not influence the number of paper clips the average consumer uses very much at all.

5. It's important to note that the slope of the demand curve and elasticity are not the same thing. Elasticity varies along a linear demand curve.

IV. **Topic 2.4: Price Elasticity of Supply**

A. *Price elasticity of supply* is the relative response of the quantity supplied to a change in price. The formula for price elasticity of supply is $Es = \dfrac{\% \text{ change in Qs}}{\% \text{ change in P}}$.

The determinant of price elasticity of supply is the time available for the product to be produced and sold. If production is time-consuming, then price elasticity of supply is *inelastic*. If producers are able to respond quickly to price changes, then price elasticity of supply is *elastic*.

1. If Es > 1, then supply is elastic. Example: plastic toys.

2. If Es < 1, then supply is inelastic. Example: fine wine.

V. **Topic 2.5: Other Elasticities**

A. *Income elasticity of demand* measures the responsiveness of quantity demanded to a change in income and is what determines whether or not goods are normal or inferior. The formula is $Ei = \% \text{ change in } \dfrac{\% \text{ change in Qd}}{\% \text{ change in Income}}$.

1. If Ei > 0, then the good is normal.

Goods are normal if an increase in income results in increased demand for the good.

2. If Ei < 0, then the good is inferior.

Goods are inferior if an increase in income results in decreased demand for the good.

B. *Cross price elasticity of demand* determines whether goods are complements or substitutes. It is the relative change in the quantity demanded of one good (x) in response to the change in price of a related good (y). The formula is $Exy = \dfrac{\% \text{ change in Qdx}}{\% \text{ change in Py}}$.

1. If Exy > 0, then the good or service is a substitute.

   Substitutes can be used in lieu of another good or service, so when the price of a substitute increases, then demand for the other good increases as consumers switch over to the cheaper alternative. For example, as ride-sharing services like Uber and Lyft have become more popular, demand for traditional taxis has decreased.

2. If Exy < 0, then the good or service is a complement.

   Goods and services that are used in conjunction with each other are considered complements. As demand for portable electronic devices increases, so does the demand for complementary goods such as phone cases, headphones, and other accessories.

VI. Topic 2.6: Market Equilibrium and Consumer and Producer Surplus

A. The market is in *equilibrium* at the point where supply and demand intersect—where quantity supplied equals quantity demanded. Equilibrium is the unique price-quantity combination at which the market "clears," meaning there is no surplus or shortage. The graph shown in Figure 4.7 illustrates a market in equilibrium. Equilibrium is identified at point E.

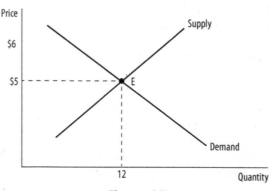

Figure 4.7

B. Consumer and Producer Surplus

1. *Consumer surplus* is the difference between the price a consumer is willing to pay and the prevailing market price. In the supply and demand model shown in Figure 4.8, it is the triangle formed underneath the demand curve above the equilibrium price. Consumer surplus can always be found below the demand curve, above the price paid and to the left of quantity purchased.

2. *Producer surplus* is the difference between the price a producer is willing to accept and the prevailing market price. In the supply and demand model below, it is the triangle formed above the supply curve and below the equilibrium price. Producer surplus can always be found above the supply (or marginal cost) curve, below the price received, and to the left of quantity sold.

3. Total economic surplus, the sum of consumer and producer surpluses, is maximized at the equilibrium price and quantity.

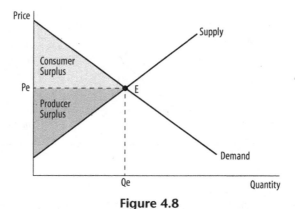

Figure 4.8

VII. **Topic 2.7: Market Disequilibrium and Changes in Equilibrium**

A. Markets do not automatically reach equilibrium. Instead, through a process of trial and error, markets eventually arrive at equilibrium. The more information that buyers and sellers have, the faster this takes place.

1. For example, if a price is higher than the market equilibrium price, as illustrated in Figure 4.9, then the amount producers offer for sale (quantity supplied) is greater than the amount consumers are willing to buy (quantity demanded) and a *surplus* results. Excess units on shelves of sellers create incentives to reduce the price which causes the quantity supplied to decrease (remember the law of supply?) and the quantity demanded to increase as consumers respond to the law of demand. Eventually this results in the surplus disappearing and the market reaching equilibrium.

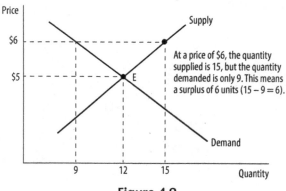

At a price of $6, the quantity supplied is 15, but the quantity demanded is only 9. This means a surplus of 6 units (15 − 9 = 6).

Figure 4.9

2. If a price is lower than the market equilibrium price (illustrated in Figure 4.10), then the amount producers offer for sale (quantity supplied) is less than the amount consumers are willing to buy (quantity demanded) and a *shortage* results. Consumers vie for the limited number available and sellers sense the shortages, driving up the price which causes the quantity demanded to decrease and the quantity supplied to increase as producers respond to the law of supply. Eventually this results in the shortage disappearing and the market reaching equilibrium.

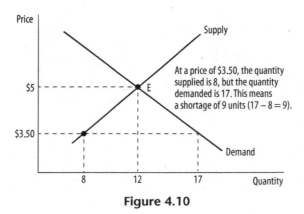

At a price of $3.50, the quantity supplied is 8, but the quantity demanded is 17. This means a shortage of 9 units (17 − 8 = 9).

Figure 4.10

Market changes are considered to happen in the "immediate short run" for the purposes of taking the AP® exam. A few questions may test your understanding of how markets get into equilibrium and why they leave shortages or surpluses when they are not there. However, the majority of questions test your ability to recognize short-run changes in equilibrium in various kinds of markets.

B. Changes in Equilibrium

1. Whenever supply or demand changes, the equilibrium price and quantity change.

2. A change in demand means that for every price there is a new quantity demanded. A change in supply means that for every price there is a new quantity supplied.

3. An increase in demand (rightward shift) results in an increase in the equilibrium price and quantity as shown in Figure 4.11. Note that this is distinct from an increase in quantity demanded because the whole function has changed (a shift of the line rather than movement along it to a new point).

4. Note that in response to the increase in demand, price rose and the quantity supplied increased (even though supply remains unchanged).

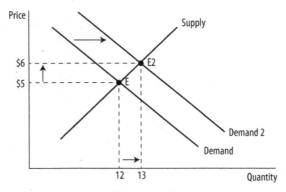

Figure 4.11

5. A decrease in demand (leftward shift) results in a decrease in the equilibrium price and quantity as illustrated in Figure 4.12. Note again the difference between this decrease in demand and the previous decrease in quantity demanded.

6. Note that as before, this causes a decrease in price and consequently a decrease in quantity supplied, though no change in the supply function.

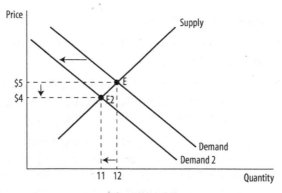

Figure 4.12

7. Changes in demand are caused by changes in consumers' tastes, consumers' incomes, the price of related goods, expected prices, and the size of the market (number of buyers). These are collectively referred to as the *determinants of demand*.

i. *Consumers' tastes* refers to a preference or a desire for a good or service. If the desire or preference increases, then demand increases. If, however, the desire or preference for the good or service decreases, then demand decreases. This determinant of demand is the right one to think of for fads, popularity due to health, coolness, or celebrity endorsement of a product, and other similar situations.

ii. *Consumers' incomes*, the amount of money they have available for buying things, affect the demand for goods and services. For most goods and services (*normal goods*), an increase in income results in an increase in demand, while a decrease in income results in a decrease in demand.

iii. There are some goods, however, for which an increase in income leads to a decrease in demand and for which a decrease in income leads to an increase in demand. These goods are called *inferior goods*. Consumers judge these goods to be inferior because when they have more income, they choose to do something else with it and buy less of these unusual goods. Nearly all goods are normal goods. Second-hand clothing, bus tickets, used cars, and generic toilet paper might be good examples of inferior goods.

iv. A change in the price of related goods can lead to a change in demand. Consumer patterns indicate that two special types of related goods have such an effect: substitutes and complements.

> ➤ *Complementary goods* are goods that are consumed together like movie tickets and popcorn or hot dogs and hot dog buns. If the price of a good increases, then the demand for the complement decreases. For example, an increase in the price of movie tickets results in a decrease in the demand for popcorn. If, however, the price of a good decreases, then the demand for the complementary good increases. For example, a decrease in the price of hot dogs results in an increase in the demand for hot dog buns.

➤ *Substitute goods* are goods that are consumed in place of each other like movie theater tickets and video rentals. If the price of a good increases, then the demand for its substitute increases. For example, an increase in the price of movie tickets results in an increase in the demand for movie rentals. If, however, the price of a substitute decreases, then the demand for the other substitute decreases. For example, a decrease in the price of movie tickets results in a decrease in the demand for movie rentals.

v. A change in expected prices results in a change in demand. If consumers expect the price of a good or service to increase, then they demand more now. If, however, they expect the price of a good or service to decrease, then they demand less now. For example, if consumers expect car prices to rise next year, then they are more likely to purchase cars this year. If consumers expect house prices to fall in the future, then they are less likely to buy a house now. Some consumers will choose to wait to take advantage of future price declines.

vi. Market size, or the number of possible consumers, affects demand. If the market size increases, then demand increases. If, however, the market size decreases, then the demand decreases. For example, if a state lowers the legal driving age from 16 to 14, then the demand for cars, gasoline, auto insurance, and wrecker services all increase.

Test Tip

A helpful mnemonic for remembering what affects demand is MERIT.

> *M – Market Size*
> *E – Expected Prices*
> *R – Related Prices*
> *I – Income*
> *T – Tastes*

8. An increase in supply (rightward shift) results in a lower equilibrium price and an increase in the equilibrium quantity

as shown in Figure 4.13. Note again the difference between this increase in supply and the previous increase in quantity supplied.

9. Note that as before, this causes a decrease in price and consequently an increase in quantity demanded, though no change in the demand function.

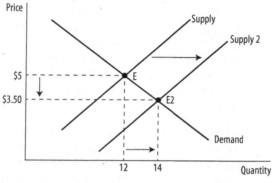

Figure 4.13

10. A decrease in supply (leftward shift) results in an increase in the equilibrium price but a lower equilibrium quantity as illustrated in Figure 4.14. Note again the difference between this decrease in supply and the previous decrease in quantity supplied.

11. Note that as before, this causes an increase in price and consequently a decrease in quantity demanded, though no change in the demand function.

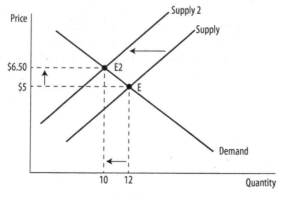

Figure 4.14

12. Changes in supply are caused by changes in the price of inputs, competition (number of firms), technology, changes in the price of related goods and services, and changes in expected prices.

    i.   If the price of inputs changes, then the ability of a producer to supply its product changes. An increase in the price of inputs results in less supply as per-unit production costs rise, while a decrease in the price of inputs results in an increase in supply as per-unit production costs fall. For example, an increase in the price of cocoa leads to a decrease in the supply of chocolate candy. A decrease in the price of coffee beans leads to an increase in the supply of coffee grounds.

    ii. More competition leads to more supply, and less competition leads to less supply. For example, if a new hamburger restaurant enters the fast-food industry, then the supply of hamburger meals increases. If a business exits an industry, then there is less supply. More suppliers means more supply!

    iii. Improvements in technology often result in an increase in the ability of producers to supply their products. The adoption of the assembly line resulted in an increase in the supply of cars during the early twentieth century just as the invention of the printing press increased the supply of books 500 years earlier.

    iv. Changes in the price of related goods and services also affect supply. When goods are produced at the same time, such as beef and leather, an increase in the price of one leads to an increase in the supply of the other, or a *complement in production* ("by-product" is pretty close).

v. More often, however, goods are produced at the expense of other goods. Consider farmers who have a fixed amount of land on which to grow crops. The decision to grow corn because it is more profitable results in a decrease in the supply of wheat and vice versa.

➤ For the Bic Corporation, plastic can be made into lighters, pens, or disposable razors. As the number of smokers has declined in recent decades, the decrease in the price of lighters has probably shifted the supply curves for pens and razors to the right. These goods that represent alternative uses of resources are called *substitutes in production.*

vi. Like consumers, producers respond to changes in expected prices. If producers expect the price of their good or service to increase, then they are less willing to offer it for sale now. However, if producers expect the price of their good to decrease, then they are more willing to offer it for sale now.

➤ For example, if gasoline producers expect prices to rise in the near future, then they may offer less for sale now and store the rest until prices increase. And certainly if people expect the value of their assets to decrease in the future, they are more willing to sell them now—just think about stocks!

Test Tip

A mnemonic that will help you to remember what causes changes in the supply of a good or service is TRICE.

T – Technology
R – Related Prices
I – Input Prices
C – Competition
E – Expected Prices

In several places on either the multiple-choice or free-response questions you will be asked to determine the effects on price and quantity of a change in either supply or demand. When presented with this type of question, it helps to have a strategy for answering the question. First, sketch a supply and demand graph in equilibrium and label the equilibrium point E. Next, determine if the question is about a change in supply or a change in demand. Look for key words that give you a clue as to whether the change involves buying or selling behavior. Anything related to buying tells you a change in demand will most likely occur. Anything related to selling or production tells you a change in supply will occur. After you have settled on which curve will shift, determine if it increases or decreases. Once again, the question will give you a clue to the direction of the change. Up, right, increase, or more are words that imply a shift of either curve to the right. Down, left, decrease, or less are words that imply a shift of the curve to the left. Now that you know the curve and the direction of the shift, sketch the change on the graph you drew earlier. Look at the new equilibrium point and label it E2. Compare the E2 to E and determine the change in price and quantity.

WARNING: There is a big exception to the advice given above. If a question ever talks about input prices or costs, then realize increases in these shift supply to the left and decreases in these shift supply to the right.

VIII. Topic 2.8: The Effects of Government Intervention in Markets

A. Sometimes governments may decide that market prices are unfair—that the market produces too much or that markets do not allocate goods and services to those desperately in need. When this is the case, governments may put price or quantity controls on the market.

B. If a government believes that a market price is too high, then it may put a *price ceiling* on a good or service. A price ceiling is a maximum price that producers and consumers are not allowed to exceed. Figure 4.15 illustrates a price ceiling and its effect on the market.

1. As shown in Figure 4.15, Pe and Qe are the market equilibrium price and quantity. Pc is the price ceiling. Qs refers to quantity supplied and Qd refers to quantity demanded. When a price ceiling is an *effective price ceiling,* it results in the quantity demanded being greater than the quantity supplied. Thus, it must be below the equilibrium price to be effective. This results in a shortage equal to Qd – Qs. Examples of price ceilings include rent controls and limits on gas prices.

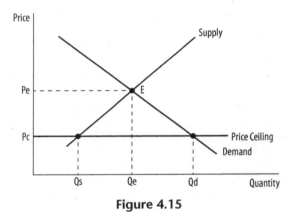

Figure 4.15

C. If a government believes that the market equilibrium price for a good is too low, it may put a *price floor* on a good or service. A price floor is a minimum price that producers and consumers are not allowed to undermine.

1. Figure 4.16 (below) illustrates a price floor and its effect on the market. In the graph, Pe and Qe are the market equilibrium price and quantity. Pf is the price floor. Qs refers to quantity supplied and Qd refers to quantity demanded. When a price floor is an *effective price floor,* it results in the quantity demanded being less than the quantity supplied. Thus, to take effect, the price floor must be above the equilibrium price. This results in a surplus equal to Qs – Qd. Examples of price floors include the minimum wage and agricultural price supports.

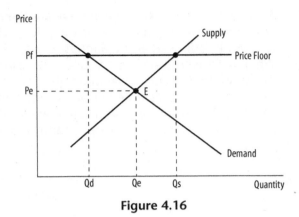

Figure 4.16

2. Figure 4.17 (below) illustrates the effect of a quota. A quota is a quantity limit. A quota is effective if it limits the quantity supplied to an amount less than the market equilibrium quantity. An effective quota results in less quantity supplied in the market at a higher price than the market equilibrium.

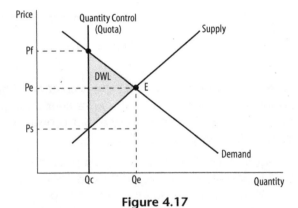

Figure 4.17

D. *Deadweight Loss* occurs whenever the market is not in equilibrium. Deadweight loss is the sum of producer and consumer surplus that could have been achieved had the equilibrium price and quantity prevailed in the market. In the previous graph on quantity control, deadweight loss was identified by area DWL.

1. In Figure 4.18, the effect of an *excise tax,* or per unit tax on production, on total surplus is shown. Ps is the price suppliers earn, Pd is the price that buyers pay. The difference between them reflects the amount of the excise tax. The area labeled *government surplus* represents the tax revenue generated by the excise tax. DWL is the area of deadweight loss created by the tax.

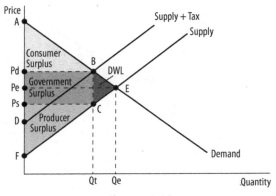

Figure 4.18

E. The incidence of a tax, or tax burden, is the percentage of the tax consumers have to pay as a higher price relative to the price before the tax. Tax incidence is dependent on the price elasticity of demand and/or the price elasticity of supply for the good or service being taxed. There is an inverse relationship between the price elasticities of demand and supply and the tax incidence on consumers. As price elasticity of demand or supply increases from perfectly inelastic to perfectly elastic, the incidence of tax on consumers decreases from 100% to 0%, so when the elasticities are relatively inelastic, consumers pay more of the tax and conversely producers pay less. But, when the elasticities of supply or demand are relatively more elastic, consumers pay less of the tax incidence while producers pay more.

F. When governments want to encourage producers to produce more of a good or service, then they may offer a per unit subsidy. A per unit subsidy offsets some of the marginal cost of production and results in an increase in supply in the market. See Figure 4.19.

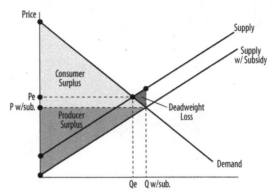

Figure 4.19

Graphs such as those found in this chapter frequently appear in the multiple-choice and free-response sections of the AP® Microeconomics exam. Be familiar with the graphs and what the different curves, areas, and points represent. For example, using Figure 4.18, determine the change in producer surplus that occurred because of the tax being imposed. Before the tax, producer surplus was triangle F, Pe, E. After the tax, producer surplus was triangle F, Ps, C. The area lost to government and deadweight loss was trapezoid Pe, E, C, Ps. Note that much, but not all, of this lost producer surplus was captured as government surplus with which it can provide a public service. Some disappeared as deadweight loss. To test yourself, see if you can repeat the process for consumer surplus with the graph shown in Figure 4.18.

IX. Topic 2.9: International Trade and Public Policy

A. When a country is open to international trade, the goods and services being either produced or consumed in the country can also be produced or consumed in other countries as well. Based on the world price of a good as determined in the worldwide market for that good, the presence of international trade may result in exports and imports.

1. Exports are goods produced domestically that are then sold outside of the country. When a domestic firm sells its good outside of the country, it is called *exporting.*

2. Refer to the graphs in Figure 4.20. The graph on the left illustrates the domestic market for a good before international trade. On the right, if the world price for a good (Pw) is higher than the domestic price (Pe), then producers have an incentive to export. The quantity exported at the world price equals the quantity supplied minus the quantity demanded in the domestic market. The result of exports is an increase in domestic producer surplus and a decrease in domestic consumer surplus.

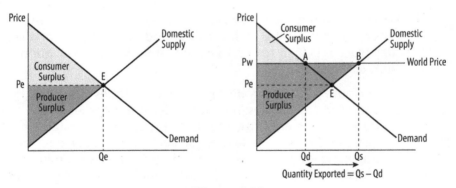

Figure 4.20

3. Imports are goods produced outside of the country that are then sold domestically. When consumers purchase goods produced outside of the country, it is called *importing.*

4. Refer to the graphs in Figure 4.21. The graph on the left illustrates the domestic market for a good before international trade. On the right, if the world price for a good (Pw) is lower than the domestic price (Pe), then consumers have an incentive to import. The quantity imported equals the quantity demanded minus the quantity being supplied domestically. The result of imports is an increase in domestic consumer surplus and a decrease in domestic producer surplus.

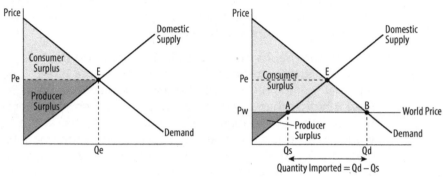

Figure 4.21

B. When a government either wants to limit competition from outside of the country and/or collect additional tax revenue, it may place a tariff, a tax on trade, on either the good or goods from other countries.

1. In Figure 4.22, the graph on the left illustrates consumer and producer surplus in a market open to international trade. On the right, the effects of a tariff are illustrated. The result of the tariff is a loss of consumer surplus equal to the trapezoid *Pw + Tariff, D, B, Pw*. The tariff results in an increase of producer surplus equal to the trapezoid *Pw + Tariff, C, A, Pw*. The tariff generates government revenue or government surplus equal to the rectangle *C, D, G, F*. Finally, the tariff creates deadweight loss equal to the areas of triangle *A, C, F* plus triangle *D, B, G*.

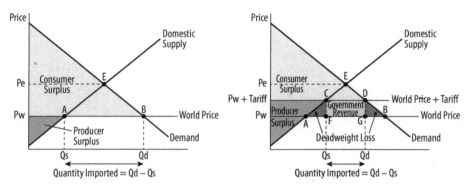

Figure 4.22

C. When a government wants to limit the amount of a good being imported from outside of the country, it may put a quantity control, such as a quota, in place. The effect of import quotas on the market is to raise the price consumers pay and to increase the quantity of domestic production relative to foreign production in the market.

UNIT 3

PRODUCTION, COST, AND THE PERFECT COMPETITION MODEL

Production and Cost

Topic 3.1: The Production Function

A. A *firm*, or business, is an individual or group of individuals who work together to produce goods and services for *profit*. Profit is the amount of money a firm gets to keep after it has paid for all of its costs or expenses.

B. Firms must decide how much of their goods or services to produce given their available land, labor, and capital. This decision begins with analysis of a firm's *production function*.

1. The production function for a firm is the amount of output, or *total product*, it can produce as it varies the use of an input. Usually this means labor. Typically, only one variable input will be analyzed at a time. Clearly, the amount produced results from labor, capital, and the current state of technology. However, we often assume that the quantity of capital available to the firm and the state of technology are fixed in the short run and that during this time the firm can alter the quantity it produces by increasing or decreasing the number of workers employed.

2. Initially, as a firm increases its use of labor (or its variable input), it experiences *increasing marginal returns*. This means that the firm's total product is increasing at a greater rate: the contribution to total product from each additional worker (unit of input) hired is higher than for the prior worker. This added contribution from employing an additional input is called *marginal product*.

3. Eventually a firm reaches a point of *diminishing marginal returns* in which total product continues to increase as the number of inputs increases, but now at a decreasing rate: the contribution of each additional input, or marginal product, is less than the one before it, but still positive.

4. Finally, the firm may experience *decreasing total returns* or negative marginal returns as total product decreases and marginal product is negative.

   i.   To understand why this happens, picture a fast-food restaurant. Initially adding a few workers to the kitchen increases the total product and marginal product for the restaurant. The workers can specialize in certain tasks, which increases productivity. Two of them may cook while the third worker takes customers' orders. Adding a fourth or fifth worker may increase the total product, but the marginal product of the fourth and fifth workers is probably less than the first three. Adding a sixth worker may result in decreasing returns since now the kitchen is overcrowded and all of the cooking equipment is probably in use by the first five workers. Beyond a certain number of employees, the fixed resources become limitations on the amount each worker can add to output. Crowding and coordination failure can eventually result in decreasing total output.

5. It is important for students taking the AP® Microeconomics exam to understand the concept of the *production function* as well as its related graph. Figure 5.1 is a graph of the production function. Notice that initially the slope of the curve is positive and increasing as inputs increase from one to three. This range of the production function shows increasing marginal returns. As inputs increase from three through five, the slope of the production function becomes positive but decreasing, showing diminishing marginal returns. As the number of inputs increase from five to six, the slope becomes negative, indicating decreasing total returns and negative marginal returns.

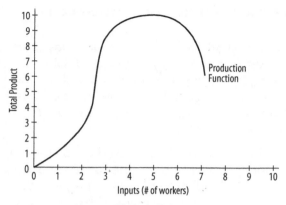

Figure 5.1

6. *Average product* is the total product divided by the number of inputs producing the total product.

   i. Using the marginal and average product graph shown below in Figure 5.2, study the relationship between the average product and the marginal product. Remember that marginal product is the change in total product that happens when a firm puts an additional employee or machine to work.

   ii. In the following graph, when marginal product is increasing, average product increases as well; as average product decreases, so does marginal product.

   iii. While marginal product is increasing, it is greater than average product, but when average product is decreasing, it is above marginal product.

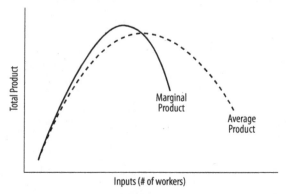

Figure 5.2

II. **Topic 3.2: Short-Run Production Costs**

A. In microeconomics, the *short run* is any time period in which at least one of a firm's inputs (land, labor, or capital) can't be changed. Usually it's capital and that accounts for the *fixed costs (FC)*. That is, the cost is unable to be changed in the short run. No matter how much total product a firm produces, its fixed costs stay the same.

1. To put it another way, fixed costs are completely independent of the firm's total product. Examples of fixed costs include: monthly rent, property taxes, salaries to managers, and payments made on loans the firm took out to purchase capital equipment.

B. Firms, or businesses, are able to change at least one input in the short run. Usually it's labor that is the variable input and accounts for (most of) the firm's *variable costs (VC)*, or the cost which firms have some control over in the short run. Unlike fixed costs, variable costs change with a firm's total product.

1. As firms produce more, their variable costs increase. As firms produce less, their variable costs shrink, all the way down to being zero when no units are produced (this is called *shutting down* in the short run). Examples of variable costs include: utility bills, income taxes, wages to hourly workers, and raw materials.

C. A firm's *total cost (TC)* is the sum of all its fixed and variable costs, which means total cost equals fixed cost plus variable cost.

$$TC = FC + VC.$$

D. Figure 5.3 illustrates fixed, variable, and total costs.

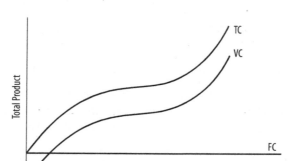

Figure 5.3

Students need to understand that the average and marginal cost curves are based on a firm's production function, average product, and marginal product. In general, the cost curves are inversely related with the product curves. The relationship between marginal and average values is always similar since marginal values are the changes in total values, and they pull averages toward the marginal value. In addition, marginal values intersect averages at the minimum or the maximum of the average function.

E. In addition to the fixed costs, variable costs, and total cost, students should be familiar with the concept of *marginal cost (MC)*. Marginal cost is the change in total cost that happens whenever a business produces one additional unit of output. It is also the slope of the total cost and variable cost curves at a particular quantity. The marginal product function (slope of production function above) determines the MC curve because the costs associated with employing one more unit of a variable input are spread over the number of units of output gained.

1. What causes a change in marginal cost? A change in variable cost leads to a change in marginal cost, but changes in fixed costs will not affect marginal cost. Marginal cost is extremely important in determining how to maximize profit for a firm,

and so it bears a very close relationship to a firm's supply decisions.

F. *Average fixed cost (AFC)* is equal to a firm's fixed cost divided by its total product. This can be expressed as $\dfrac{FC}{Q}$. Initially, AFC for a firm is really big, but as a firm increases its output while its fixed costs remain the same, the AFC gets closer and closer to zero, approaching, but never touching, the *x*-axis.

G. *Average variable cost (AVC)* is a firm's variable cost divided by its total product. This can be expressed as $\dfrac{VC}{Q}$. Initially, AVC for a firm is high, then it decreases, but eventually it increases because marginal cost is increased.

H. *Average total cost (ATC)* is the sum of the firm's AFC and AVC. ATC = AFC + AVC. Notice in Figure 5.4 that as output increases, ATC initially decreases because of increasing returns, but eventually it increases because of diminishing marginal returns. In the graph below, also notice how ATC and AVC get closer together as the quantity increases. This happens because AFC is getting smaller and smaller as a firm increases production.

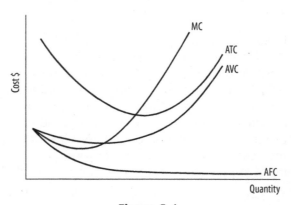

Figure 5.4

Students taking the AP® Microeconomics exam should be very familiar with the average and marginal cost curves. They should be able to reproduce them for the free-response questions. Multiple-choice questions on cost curves often have students demonstrate that they understand the relationships between the different curves. For example, a question may test a student's understanding of the relationship between variable and marginal cost, or a question may test a student's understanding of what's happening to ATC given a certain position on the firm's MC curve. Given that AFC is the distance between AVC and ATC, it is often not shown on a graph.

To test yourself: Practice drawing MC, ATC, and AVC (without peeking) so that

➤ *MC looks like a swoosh;*

➤ *It intersects AVC and ATC at each of their minimum points;*

➤ *ATC and AVC get closer and closer together but never touch.*

This typically takes students many, many tries before it becomes second nature. It is an acquired skill and can be learned with practice. It will be worth your time. Most AP® Microeconomics exams require that these three curves be drawn at some point in the free-response section.

III. Topic 3.3: Long-Run Production Costs

A. The *long run* happens when firms can change *all* of their inputs. All costs are variable in the long run. Unlike the short run in which a firm may only be able to hire more workers in response to demand for its product, in the long run, a firm can increase not only the number of workers, but also the number of machines, the size of its factory, and even the way it does business.

B. In the series of graphs (Figures 5.5, 5.6, and 5.7), you can see many different *short-run* ATC (average total cost) curves that could exist as a firm grows in size. At first, the SRATC curves get lower as the firm gets bigger, then it levels out. Finally, the

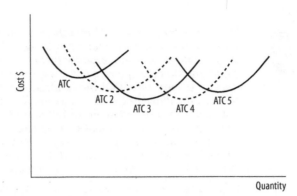

Figure 5.5

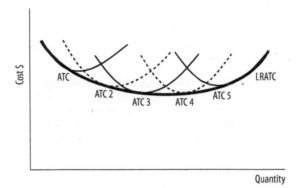

Figure 5.6

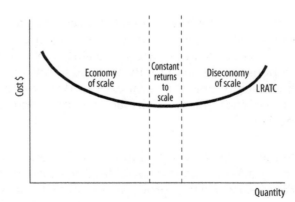

Figure 5.7

SRATC curves get higher as the firm gets even bigger. What you are seeing are different *economies of scale*. Combining the minimum points of all of the ATC curves that could exist gives us the *long-run average total cost curve (LRATC)*.

1. Look at Figure 5.7. The region of the LRATC left of both dashed lines illustrates economy of scale. *Economies of scale* means that increasing the size of the firm results in lower average total cost, which is productively efficient. This happens because as firms become larger, the marginal product of labor increases.

2. The region of Figure 5.7 to the right of both dashed lines shows a *diseconomy of scale*. Diseconomies of scale happen when firms become too big and they stop being productively efficient as their average total cost increases.

3. *Constant returns to scale* can be seen between the dashed lines in Figure 5.7. In this case, the constant returns to scale occur as the firm's average total cost ranges from ATC 3 to ATC 4. Notice in Figure 5.5 that the minimum of ATC 3 and ATC 4 are the same. Constant returns to scale may occur if increasing a firm's size neither decreases nor increases its average total cost.

The Perfect Competition Model

Topic 3.4: Types of Profit

A. A *profit* happens whenever a firm makes more money (*revenue*) from producing and selling a good or service than it spends in producing and selling the same good or service.

B. An *accounting profit* exists when the amount of revenue is greater than the explicit or clearly seen costs of production. Recall that explicit costs are money payments made to others for use of factors of production not owned by the business owner.

    1. For example, if an accountant opens a small neighborhood tattoo parlor and earns revenue of $1000 while spending $100 on ink, needles, and a city permit, then the accountant earned an accounting profit of $1000 − $100 = $900.

C. An *economic profit* exists when the amount of revenue is greater than both the explicit costs and implicit costs (opportunity costs) of production.

    1. For example, assume that the accountant mentioned above faces the same scenario, but this time wants to see if he or she has made an economic profit. To find the economic profit, the accountant takes the accounting profit of $900 and subtracts the opportunity cost. What's the opportunity cost? It is the value of the resources, particularly the labor, of the business owner that the accountant chose to sacrifice by not working in another capacity. If the accountant could have instead gone to his or her office and earned $900 for

Chapter 6

the day, then the $900 the accountant could have earned is the opportunity cost. So, $900 in accounting profits minus $900 in opportunity costs means that the accountant has earned zero economic profit.

D. In economics, a firm is making a *normal profit* when its economic profit is zero.

   1. A firm earning a normal profit is making just enough profit to keep the entrepreneur from leaving the industry and entering another industry, but not enough so that new firms are tempted to rush to join the industry.

E. Economic profits are important because their presence is a signal for other firms to enter into the market and compete with existing firms.

   1. If firms in an industry are earning a normal profit, then no incentive exists for the firms to exit and for other firms to enter.

   2. If a firm is earning less than a normal profit (taking an economic loss), then the firm should leave the industry.

   3. Keep in mind (when looking at economics graphs) that areas of profit represent economic profits or losses. When it looks on a graph as though the firm is breaking even, it is making exactly a normal profit and there will be no tendency for the industry to grow or shrink.

II. Topic 3.5: Profit Maximization

A. Firms make the biggest (maximum) profits when the amount of revenue they earn from producing an additional unit of output (*marginal revenue*) equals the cost of producing the additional unit of output (*marginal cost*). To see why that is, look at Figure 6.1, which compares the total revenue of a firm with its total cost.

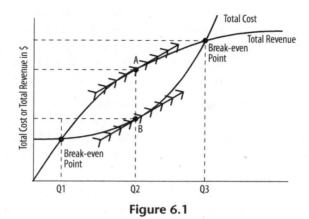

Figure 6.1

1. As a firm produces more and more output, it experiences various levels of profit and loss. In the graph above, when the firm produces quantity Q1, both its total revenue and total cost are equal. This means that the firm is earning zero economic profit (exactly normal profit), or is breaking even.

2. As the firm increases output from Q1 to Q2, notice what happens to the slope of the total revenue curve and the total cost curve. Initially, the rate of change in total revenue (marginal revenue) is greater than the rate of change in total cost (marginal cost), so the TR curve rises faster than the TC curve.

   i. When the firm reaches an output of quantity Q2, the rate at which total revenue is changing (marginal revenue) is equal to the rate at which total cost is changing (marginal cost).

      ➤ This is seen as points A and B. The arrowed lines represent the slopes of each curve at these points. The slope of the line going through point A is the same thing as the firm's marginal revenue. The slope of the line going through point B is the same thing as the firm's marginal cost.

> ➤ When marginal revenue equals marginal cost, total revenue is at its greatest relative to total cost. The vertical distance between TR and TC (from point A down to point B) is the maximum profit that the firm can possibly earn in the short run.

    ii. If the firm were to increase its output from Q2 toward Q3, the profit would shrink as the marginal revenue diminishes and the marginal cost increases. Note that TC is rising more rapidly than TR in this section of the graph.

    iii. The vertical distance between TR and TC is shrinking as the firm's profits, while still positive, decline. At Q3, the firm reaches its second break-even point where its total revenue and total cost are equal.

    iv. Beyond Q3, the firm's total cost is greater than the firm's total revenue. The vertical distance (TR – TC) is actually negative and the firm is taking an economic loss.

B. A firm maximizes profits when marginal revenue (MR) equals marginal cost (MC). This is true for every firm regardless of whether it's a small lemonade stand or a large multinational corporation.

    1. Profit maximization happens when MR = MC no matter the market structure.

    2. For some firms, it may be the case that they can't make a profit or manage to break even at any quantity. In those cases, the firm would be expected to try to minimize its losses.

    3. The phrase *profit maximization* should be interpreted to cover these situations as well. The firm's task is the same because it is still trying to maximize profit (TR – TC) even if the unfortunate reality for it is that the maximum value is a negative profit.

The majority of the AP® Microeconomics exam focuses on the different market structures. It's important to know that the profit-maximizing condition is always found at the quantity where MR = MC regardless of the amount of competition a firm faces. The following figure is included to show how the different market structures relate to one another.

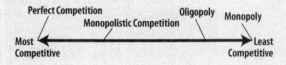

III. Topic 3.6: Firms' Short-Run Decisions to Produce and Long-Run Decisions to Enter or Exit a Market

A. Changes in the market supply or demand for a product will cause the firm to either earn economic profits or encounter economic losses.

   1. The side-by-side graphs in Figure 6.2 show how an increase in market demand affects the firm in the short run.

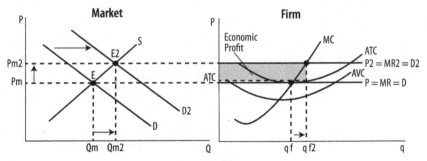

Figure 6.2

i.   In the market graph on the left, the increase in demand from D to D2 tugs the market into a new equilibrium, E2. There has been an increase in the market price from Pm to Pm2 and an increase in quantity from Qm to Qm2.

ii. The new equilibrium-market price (Pm2) becomes the price the firm takes and as a result is also the firm's marginal revenue (MR2) and new demand curve (D2).

iii. The firm produces at the point where MR2 = MC to maximize profits. This results in the firm increasing production from q f to q f2. At that quantity, the firm earns economic profits (shaded area) in the short run because the price is greater than the firm's average total cost (ATC). Note carefully where the profit box is. It will always have a height of price minus average total cost (P – ATC) and always have a width of the quantity the firm produces (the q for which MC = MR).

iv. Although the firm is allocatively efficient (P2 = MC at the quantity the firm makes – q2), it is not productively efficient because at quantity q f2 it is not producing at the lowest ATC.

2. In the long run, the presence of economic profits in the industry gives other entrepreneurs an incentive to enter into the industry and compete with the firms already there. The side-by-side graphs in Figure 6.3 show how the market and firm adjust to the long run.

i.   In the market graph, the entrance of the new firms (one of the determinants of supply) is seen as the increase in the supply curve from S to S2. This results in a new equilibrium (E3). At E3, the price returns to the previous market price of Pm while the quantity produced increases from Qm2 to Qm because of the additional firms adding to the already existing output.

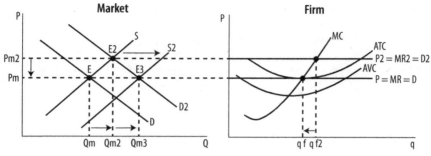

Figure 6.3

ii. The firm sees its economic profits disappear as the market price and therefore the firm's demand and marginal revenue return to their original level.

iii. As always, the firm maximizes profits by producing where MR = MC and so returns to producing quantity qf. Note that each firm produces a smaller quantity after this long-run adjustment but that the market quantity increases due to the increased number of firms.

iv. Note that as before, when in long-run equilibrium, the firm is allocatively and productively efficient once again.

3. Will a firm produce if it is taking an economic loss? It depends. If the firm can at least cover its variable costs, it will remain in business. However, if a firm is unable to earn enough to at least cover its variable costs, then the firm will shut down. In the long run, firms may not just shut down, but exit the industry entirely.

4. In Figures 6.4 and 6.5, a decrease in market demand resulted in a lower market price and quantity. The market demand decrease also resulted in the firm facing a lower price, lower marginal revenue, and less demand.

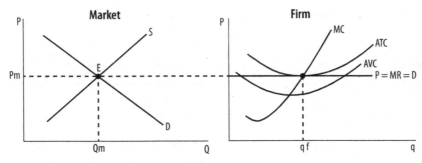

Figure 6.4

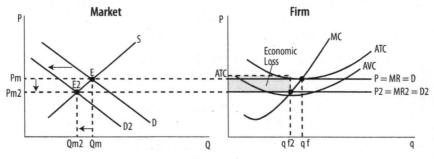

Figure 6.5

i.   In the short run, the firm earns an economic loss. Should it shut down? No, as long as the price is equal to or greater than AVC, then the firm should continue to operate in the short run.

ii.   Why should a firm operate if it's taking a loss? When a firm is operating above AVC, then it is at least covering its variable costs and maybe even some of its fixed costs. If the firm shuts down, then its loss will be greater than if it were to continue.

iii.   In Figure 6.6 a firm is operating at a price equal to its average variable cost. In review, a firm operating below point A and above point B should continue to produce in the short run. Below point B, the firm should shut down.

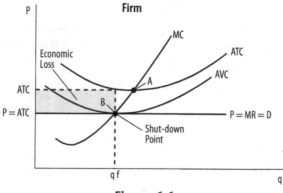

Figure 6.6

5. The firm's marginal cost curve from point B and up is also the firm's supply curve. In general, a competitive firm's short-run individual supply curve is its MC above AVC.

6. How does the presence of economic losses affect firms in the long run? The graphs below illustrate the long-run response to losses in an industry as some firms exit.

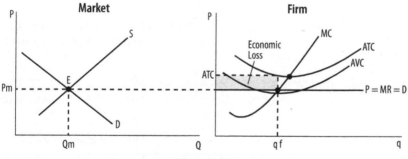

Figure 6.7

7. As some firms exit the industry because of economic losses, the market supply decreases. This results in a higher market price (Pm2) but lower market quantity (Qm2).

8. The higher market price means an increase in the firm's marginal revenue and demand. This results in a return to the long-run equilibrium in which the firm earns a normal profit and is both allocatively efficient (P = MC) and productively efficient (q at ATC minimum).

B. Costs in the Long Run

1. In the long run, perfectly competitive firms face different average total costs depending on the industry they compete in.

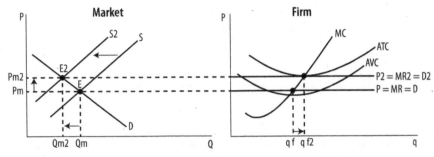

Figure 6.8

i. Constant costs across an industry occur when the number of firms in the industry has no effect on each individual firm's average total cost. Whether the firm is new or has been around awhile it has no effect on each firm's average total cost.

> ➤ For example, farmers face the same average total cost regardless of the time they have spent in the industry.

ii. Increasing costs across an industry happens when the entrance of new firms drives up the cost of inputs used by the entire industry.

> ➤ For example, as more hotels are built along a popular beach, newer firms face ever-increasing costs as scarce beachfront property becomes increasingly expensive.

iii. Decreasing costs across an industry happens when the entrance of new firms drives down the cost of inputs used by the entire industry.

> ➤ As tablet computers become more popular,
> the firms that supply the glass and lightweight
> components to the tablet industry expand and
> experience economies of scale, which reduces the
> cost of inputs for the tablet industry as a whole.

IV. Topic 3.7: Perfect Competition

A. *Perfect competition* exists when both buyers and sellers are price takers. That means neither has any influence over the price of a product.

B. Conditions for perfect competition

1. There are so many sellers that no single seller's contribution to the industry's output is significant. Sellers can sell any quantity they want at a market price that is determined outside their control. This is what it means to be a price taker, and it means that from the firm's perspective, demand is a perfectly elastic horizontal line.

2. Producers all offer an identical product or *commodity*. In perfect competition, consumers don't care from which seller they buy the product because all of the producers are offering the exact same thing.

    i. *Homogenous* and *undifferentiated* are terms frequently used to describe this same idea. For example, most people don't care which farmer produced the wheat or corn they eat. Because the goods are identical, there is no *non-price competition* between firms claiming to have better products than each other.

3. Producers are able to enter into and exit from the market freely. This means that they don't face any *barriers to entry*. Based on your understanding of economic profit, you'd probably guess if entrepreneurs could expect to make positive economic profits in an industry, that new firms would be joining that industry over time.

i.   The opposite happens when firms in a sector are taking losses—some go under in the long run. Whether there are barriers to entry in an industry dictates whether firms will be able to make economic profits in the long run. In this case, since there are no barriers to market entry and exit, firms can be expected to break even or make exactly a normal profit in the long run.

C. Graphing Perfect Competition

1.   Students must be able to graph perfect competition and understand how changes in market prices and other variables affect a perfectly competitive firm in both the short run and long run. Because each firm is such a small portion of the market, there are separate graphs for the market (in which all buyers and sellers interact to determine the overall quantity and price) and for a sample firm (in which an individual price-taking business decides how many units to produce based on its costs). These graphs should be drawn side-by-side in order to properly transfer information from one to the other.

2.   Figure 6.9 shows a market for an industry (left) and an individual firm (right) in a long-run equilibrium.

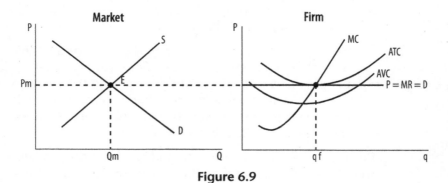

Figure 6.9

i.   The price determined in the market (Pm) becomes the demand curve and the marginal revenue curve the firm faces.

ii.   The firm uses the profit maximization rule (MR = MC) to determine its profit maximizing output of (q f).

iii. In this case, a long-run equilibrium is shown because the firm is only earning a normal profit (zero economic profit).

iv.   The firm is productively efficient because it is producing at the lowest average total cost (ATC).

v.   The firm is allocatively efficient because it is producing at the point where the marginal cost equals the market price.

You should be able to reproduce the side-by-side market and firm graphs from memory for the free-response section of the exam. Pay careful attention to labeling the curves as these are some of the easiest points to earn on the free-response section of the AP® Microeconomics exam.

UNIT 4

IMPERFECT COMPETITION

Monopoly

I. Topic 4.1: Introduction to Imperfectly Competitive Markets

A. A market is *imperfect* when one of the conditions for perfect competition is not met. For example, if instead of many sellers, a market has just a few or one, then the market behaves differently and is considered imperfect.

B. In the *product market*, imperfect competition includes: monopoly, oligopoly, and monopolistic competition. In the *factor market*, imperfect competition includes monopsony.

C. Imperfectly competitive product markets can be described by how many sellers exist in the market and by how much control individual firms have over the price of goods in the market.

D. Unlike perfect competition, imperfectly competitive firms have a degree of power to change the price.

  1. This pricing power is offset by the fact that in order to sell more of a good, they must still lower the price.

  2. The ability to control prices leads to a condition in the market where the price does not necessarily reflect the marginal cost of production.

E. Another difference between perfectly competitive and imperfectly competitive markets is the presence of *barriers to entry*.

  1. High startup costs, government regulations, and control over certain factors of production are examples of barriers which limit the ability of new firms to enter into imperfectly competitive markets.

II. Topic 4.2: Monopoly

A. A *monopoly* is when there is only one firm supplying the market with a unique good or service.

B. Monopoly markets have *barriers to entry* which keep new firms from entering the monopolized market and competing.

C. Because they don't face competition from other firms, monopolists have a lot of power over price and quantity in their particular market limited only by consumers' demand. This makes monopolies very different from firms in perfect competition that have no control over the price at which their goods can be sold.

D. Monopolies lie at the extreme opposite end of the market-structure spectrum from perfect competition.

Test Tip *AP® exam questions that explicitly or implicitly require comparison or contrast between perfect competition and monopolies are quite common.*

E. A *geographic monopoly* exists when a business has no competition in a certain geographic area. For example, in the desert southwest of the United States, a remote small town might have only one gasoline station. Because this station lacks any local competition, it's able to charge a significantly higher price for gasoline than stations that face local competition.

F. A *government monopoly* exists when only the government provides a certain good or service. Today, unlike the past, only the Federal Reserve System may issue the currency you're familiar with, the dollar.

    1. Prior to the American Civil War, almost any bank or business could issue currency.

    2. In Mexico, the government owns all of the gasoline stations and operates them under the name PEMEX.

G. A *natural monopoly* exists when the industry features such extreme economies of scale that one firm can serve the market more cheaply than any combination of smaller firms.

    1. Utility companies that provide electricity or water service to a region are examples of a natural monopoly. We will explore natural monopolies further at the end of this chapter.

H. A *technological monopoly* exists when the government grants a *patent* or *copyright* to an individual or firm.

    1. A patent protects an individual's/firm's invention or process from being legally copied by another person or firm for a fixed period of time.

        i.   Patents encourage innovation and invention by giving the inventor an opportunity to earn monopoly profits while the patent is in effect.

        ii.   For example, patents provide an incentive for pharmaceutical companies to spend millions of dollars inventing new drugs to treat or cure many diseases and conditions in the hope that they will earn billions of dollars by being the only firm legally able to produce the new medicine.

    2. A copyright gives an author or artist the monopoly over their intellectual property for at least their lifetime.

I. Because the monopolist is the only firm in its particular market, it faces the entire down-sloping market demand curve where it only produces in the elastic (upper-half) region of the demand curve to maximize profits.

J. Look at Figure 7.1, which follows. The graph shows the demand and marginal revenue curves a monopolist faces. Why is marginal revenue below the demand curve? As the monopolist tries to sell more output, it must lower its price on each additional unit and also on each previous unit. For example, if a monopolist wants to go from selling 300 units to selling 301 units, then it must lower its price on all of its output. This means that the additional revenue generated decreases at an ever-faster rate as the monopolist lowers its price to meet consumer demand.

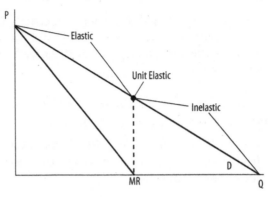

Figure 7.1

Be able to explain that a single-price monopolist produces only in the elastic range of the demand curve because at any quantity for which MR is negative, TR is lower and because TC is a continuously increasing function.

K. The Profit Maximization Rule

1. Like perfectly competitive firms, monopolists maximize profits by producing up to the point where the marginal revenue of production equals the marginal cost of production.

2. However, monopolies have an extra step that they very much enjoy. Note that after they determine the quantity (Q, below where MC = MR) they *seek* or *search* to find the price at which that quantity is demanded. This two-step process is different from perfect competitors' one-step job of picking a quantity and is common to all firms that are not price takers. (In fact they may be accurately called *price seekers* or *price searchers*.)

3. Where did AVC go? It's still there, but from here on it's not relevant to understanding the rest of the market structures. So, goodbye, AVC!

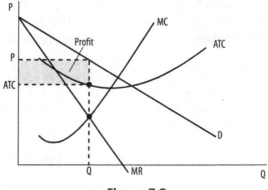

Figure 7.2

L. Productive Inefficiency

   1. A monopoly is not productively efficient because it does not produce at the lowest average total cost.

   2. Study Figure 7.3 below and notice the difference between where the monopoly produces and the minimum point of ATC.

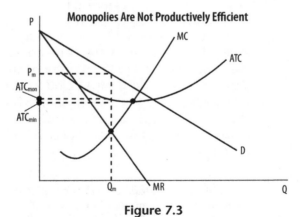

Figure 7.3

M. Allocative Inefficiency

   1. A monopoly is not allocatively efficient because the monopoly price is greater than the marginal cost of production. The gap between Qm, the monopolist's output, and Qc, the

allocatively efficient output that would be achieved if the industry had many producers, shows the under-allocation that resulted from this market having only one seller.

2. Figure 7.4 illustrates the deadweight loss created by the monopoly not being allocatively efficient. Pm refers to the monopoly price while Pc refers to the competitive price. Notice that Pc equals marginal cost (MC), while Pm is greater than MC at Qm.

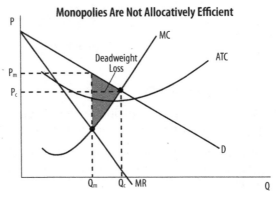

Figure 7.4

i. Deadweight loss resulting from underproduction will always be found below the demand curve, above marginal cost, and to the right of quantity produced. If you see it as a rightward-pointing arrow, it may help you double-check your work on problems involving deadweight loss, because it will always *point* you right at the socially optimal (or allocatively efficient) level of production.

Test Tip

Be sure to understand the efficiency differences between perfect competition and monopoly. Perfect competition in the long run is both productively efficient (Quantity = minimum ATC) and allocatively efficient (Price = MC). Monopolists are both productively and allocatively inefficient. Why? They're not productively efficient because the quantity produced is not at minimum ATC and the monopolist's price is greater than MC.

III. Topic 4.3: Price Discrimination

A. *Price discrimination* is the ability of some monopolists to charge consumers different prices for the same good or service.

1. Several conditions must be true for price discrimination to occur.

    i.   The firm must have some ability to set the price. For example, monopolists have pricing power because they don't face competition from other firms.

    ii. The firm must be able to prevent customers from reselling the firm's products or services to other consumers. For example, airlines print customers' names on tickets to prevent other consumers from using them. Some firms offer warranties in order to get consumers to register their products for the same reason.

    iii. The firm must be able to differentiate customers either individually or by groups so that it can charge them different amounts. Your local movie theater probably charges students a lower price than they charge teachers to see the same movie. The firm is separating people into groups based on willingness to pay, or elasticity. In the extreme, if a firm can charge each individual a different price for the same good or service, then *perfect price discrimination* exists.

    iv. The following graphs (Figure 7.5) illustrate a single-price monopolist and a monopolist that practices perfect-price discrimination. Notice that demand equals marginal revenue for the firm able to perfectly discriminate. Also, notice how consumer surplus and deadweight loss vanish when the firm can perfectly price discriminate.

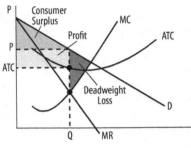

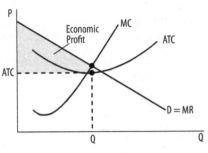

Figure 7.5

IV. Natural Monopoly Revisited

A. Recall from earlier in the chapter that natural monopolies have economies of scale so their large size effectively prevents competition from smaller (and thus higher ATC) firms, serving as a barrier to entry into the market. The example of natural monopoly mentioned previously in the chapter was a utility company that generates electricity.

B. Figure 7.6 isn't all that different from the monopoly graphs we've examined earlier. The big exception is the shape of MC and ATC, which reflect the large firm size with a very low marginal cost, meaning that ATC is always decreasing as quantity increases (because MC is below it).

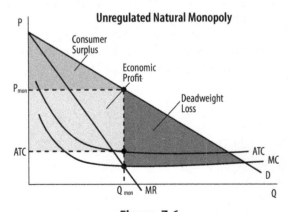

Figure 7.6

C. Note the large areas of deadweight loss and economic profit in Figure 7.6. From a society's point of view, this large DWL is undesirable. However, unlike other monopolies which can be broken into parts (*trustbusting* is a term to describe what was done to Standard Oil or Bell Telephone), natural monopolies would not be good choices for this strategy since any combination of smaller firms would be less productively efficient (there would be higher ATC and MC curves).

D. Governments regulate utilities' prices so that the utilities don't use their monopoly power to charge monopoly prices.

1. Why does government allow a natural monopoly to operate?

2. A natural monopoly has an economy of scale which means that it produces at a much lower average total cost (ATC) than multiple smaller firms producing the same amount of output.

3. Government regulation is prompted by the desire to reduce or eliminate deadweight loss resulting from underproduction.

4. Government promotes productive efficiency by allowing the natural monopoly with its lower ATC to operate, and it promotes allocative efficiency by regulating the monopoly's price.

5. In Figures 7.7 through 7.9, compare the differences between the unregulated and the regulated natural monopoly. The subscript *a.e.* that appears in the graphs refers to the concept of *allocative efficiency*. The subscript *p.e.* refers to *productive efficiency*.

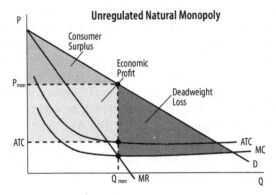

Figure 7.7

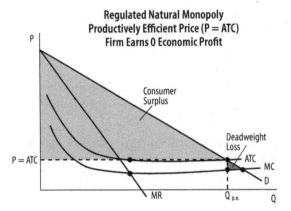

Figure 7.8

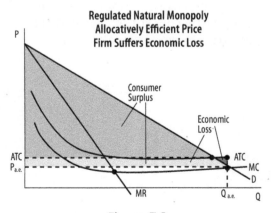

Figure 7.9

Monopolistic Competition

Chapter 8

I. Topic 4.4: Monopolistic Competition

A. *Monopolistic competition* is a market structure that has similarities with both *perfect competition* and *monopoly*. In addition, it has its own unique features. An example of a monopolistically-competitive industry that will help your understanding of the concept is the fast-food industry.

1. Monopolistic competition's similarities with perfect competition:

   i.   There are many firms competing against each other. For example, there are hundreds, if not thousands, of firms in the fast-food industry.

   ii. The barriers to entry are very low, so it's relatively easy for new firms to enter into monopolistically-competitive markets.

   iii. In the short run, it's possible to earn economic profit, but in the long run, economic profits attract competition and disappear.

2. Monopolistic competition's similarities with monopoly:

   i.   Monopolistically-competitive firms have the ability to set a price for their product, though they have a narrower range of prices they can choose, so changing prices affects quantity sold proportionally more than for a monopolist.

ii. They face a downward-sloping demand curve for their product because of their pricing power, but the demand curve is flatter than a monopolist's—they usually face a more elastic demand curve than do monopolists.

iii. Because they face a downward-sloping demand curve, the marginal revenue is less than demand.

3. Features unique to monopolistic competition:

i. So that they can earn an economic profit, monopolistically-competitive firms make products that are different (or are presented as being different) than their competitors' products. Efforts on behalf of a firm to distinguish its products from potential competitors' output are called *product differentiation*. Firms do this to make other goods seem less substitutable for their own, allowing them to charge higher prices and not lose as much market share.

   ➤ For example, McDonald's, Burger King, Wendy's, Dairy Queen, Sonic, and Jack in the Box all make hamburgers, but each tries to differentiate their burgers from the competition. McDonald's offers the multi-layered Big Mac while Burger King is the home of the flame-broiled Whopper, and so on.

ii. Monopolistically-competitive firms spend some of their scarce resources on advertising their products. This means that they must sacrifice production in order to spend money on advertising. They do this to attract new consumers and to create brand loyalty for their existing customers. Firms use advertising to point out the real and/or perceived differences between their products and those of the competition, reinforcing the goal of product differentiation.

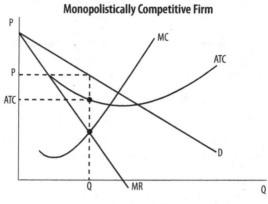

Figure 8.1

Be able to graph monopolistic competition in both a short-run and long-run equilibrium. Also, make sure you can identify the profit-maximizing quantity and price (Q and P in the graph above). For the short-run equilibrium graph above, note the similarities with the graph of monopoly in short-run profit. The only real difference in how you should draw it is that the D and MR curves have a little less slope downward than in a monopoly graph.

B. Product differentiation allows, but does not guarantee, that monopolistically-competitive firms will earn economic profits in the short run.

C. Product differentiation results in a market for the firm's particular output, so the firm's demand and marginal revenue are downward sloping.

D. The monopolistically-competitive firm, along with perfectly-competitive firms and monopolists, maximizes profits by producing the quantity associated with marginal revenue equaling marginal cost.

E. Monopolistically-competitive firms are inefficient in the short run.

1. They are productively inefficient because they don't produce a quantity of output associated with average total cost (ATC) being at its lowest point.

2. They are allocatively inefficient because the price earned by the firm is not equal to its marginal cost of production.

3. Because they are not allocatively efficient, monopolistic competition results in deadweight loss.

4. Figure 8.2 illustrates the consumer surplus, economic profit, and deadweight loss associated with monopolistic competition.

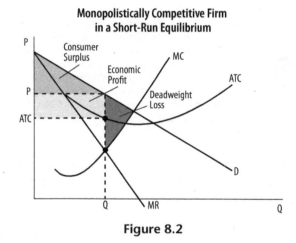

Figure 8.2

i. Look at the firm's ATC curve and notice its average total cost compared to the minimum. It's not productively efficient.

ii. Notice the firm's quantity of output. It's much less than that associated with a perfectly competitive market (MC = D).

It's important that you be able to identify the areas of surplus, profit, and deadweight loss for all market structures.

F. The two graphs below (Figure 8.3 and Figure 8.4) illustrate the effects of competition from new firms on a monopolistically-competitive firm earning an economic profit.

Monopolistically Competitive Firm in the Short Run

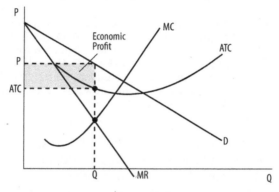

Figure 8.3

Monopolistically Competitive Firm in the Long Run

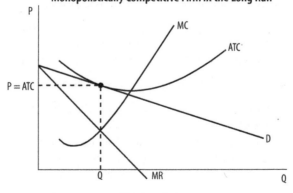

Figure 8.4

1. Figure 8.3 shows the monopolistically-competitive firm earning an economic profit.

2. The presence of economic profits (P > ATC) is an incentive for new firms to enter the market and compete.

3. Figure 8.4 shows that eventually, as new firms enter and compete, demand for the existing firm's product decreases (and when demand shifts left, so does marginal revenue) until a long-run equilibrium is reached in which no firms earn economic profit.

Test Tip

Monopolistic competition in the long run can be a difficult graph to draw. The key to drawing it is to add the ATC curve last. Draw D, MR, and MC first. Identify the profit maximizing quantity where MR = MC. Next, draw a dotted line down to the horizontal axis and then up to the demand curve and make a point. Finally, draw ATC so that it is tangent to the demand curve at the point.

4. Unlike perfect competition, the long-run equilibrium is neither productively efficient (quantity is not at minimum ATC) nor allocatively efficient (the price is greater than the marginal cost and deadweight loss exists).

G. Monopolistically-competitive firms do not produce enough output to achieve the lowest ATC possible.

1. When compared to perfectly-competitive firms, monopolistically-competitive firms of similar size and with similar costs produce less output in the long run.

2. This problem is called *excess capacity*.

3. In Figure 8.5, Q' is the quantity perfectly-competitive firms would produce in the long run which is at the lowest ATC. Q is the quantity produced by a monopolistically-competitive firm. The difference between them is excess capacity. Excess capacity is evidence that the firm is not

productively efficient. *Q'* represents the optimal use of this factory size. Because the firm is producing at less than the. optimal level for its scale of plant, it experiences a higher ATC than minimum.

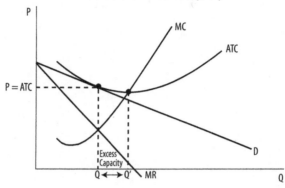

The Problem of Excess Capacity

Figure 8.5

Oligopoly and Game Theory

Topic 4.5: Oligopoly

A. *Oligopoly* is a market structure in which just a few firms dominate the market. Examples of oligopolistic markets include the breakfast-cereal industry, automobile industry, airline industry, and cellular-phone industry.

B. In oligopoly, it is difficult for new firms to enter into the market and compete because there are barriers to entry.

1. Economies of scale give existing firms a low-cost advantage over newer, smaller entrants into the market.

2. Existing firms may cooperate to prevent new firms from entering the market.

3. Existing firms enjoy huge name recognition due to their size and prominence.

C. Firms act *interdependently*. This means that the firms' best choices are influenced by one another's decisions, an aspect that introduces an element of strategy into the way firms behave.

1. Because there are so few competitors in oligopoly, firms have to be strategic in their production and pricing decisions. This means they carefully consider the possible decisions and reactions of other firms when deciding how much to produce or at what price to offer their output for sale.

2. Often this dependence is two-way, as in the case of Coke and Pepsi, when deciding how many units to produce or what price to charge.

3. In some oligopolies, because firms are of unequal size, one firm is recognized as the price leader, and other firms set their prices in response to the leading firm. The ketchup market is a good example of the price-leadership type of oligopoly, with Heinz acting as the dominant firm.

D. Oligopolistic firms can either produce similar or differentiated products depending on the industry in which they compete.

E. Oligopolistic firms have an incentive to *collude*, or illegally cooperate, to set prices and production.

F. Left unregulated, collusion among firms may result in them forming a *cartel*, which is a formal agreement to not compete, but instead behave as a monopoly by collectively determining quantity and price rather than doing so separately.

1. Collusion, price-fixing, and other behaviors indicative of formation of cartels are highly regulated in the United States and many other countries.

   ➤ An example of a cartel is the Organization of Petroleum Exporting Countries (OPEC). OPEC colludes to limit oil production and thus set the price of oil higher than it otherwise would be if member nations each acted to maximize profits.

G. This tendency toward cartel formation also faces a natural limitation: firms often have an incentive to "cheat" on the quantity and price decisions that were collectively reached. This incentive to cheat can be illustrated and analyzed using certain types of games, and this is why much of the study of oligopoly involves game theory.

II. Topic 4.5 (continued): Game Theory

A. Unlike other market structures that are modeled graphically, oligopoly can be modeled using a tool from game theory called a *payoff matrix.*

   1. Game theory is the study of strategic decision-making. *Games* in this context refers to strategic situations in which a discrete number of players face choices that result in quantifiable benefits to each.

   2. A payoff matrix is a grid that shows the possible combinations of outcomes (benefits) when two people or firms make decisions in such a game.

B. Look at the following payoff matrix and determine the possible daily profit two firms could earn given their choice to set a high price or a low price. Assume the firms both try to maximize their profit and know all of the information in the payoff matrix.

	Firm A High Price	Firm A Low Price
Firm B High Price	A: $1000 B: $1000	A: $1200 B: $ 500
Firm B Low Price	A: $ 500 B: $1200	A: $ 750 B: $ 750

Test Tip

Make sure to understand how a payoff matrix works. You will see one or more in the multiple-choice section and/or the free-response section of the exam.

C. What can you learn about a firm's incentives by studying a payoff matrix?

    1. If the firms compete, then they would both charge a low price and earn a daily profit of $750. Why?

        i. Because the low-price strategy is a *dominant strategy* in this situation.

        ii. A dominant strategy is the one a profit-maximizing firm pursues independent of the other firm's strategy.

> For example, Firm A is always better off choosing a low-price strategy. If firm B sets a high price, then firm A makes a bigger profit choosing low ($1200) than it would by setting a high price ($1000). Also, if firm B sets a low price, then firm A still makes a bigger profit choosing low ($750) than it would by setting a high price ($500). For firm A, the low price strategy dominates the high-price strategy because it is the best response *no matter what the opposing firm chooses.*

        iii. Repeat this analysis to find that choosing a low price is also a dominant strategy for firm B. In this case, the result is the same, but on some problems one firm (or even both) may not have a dominant strategy.

        iv. When one strategy is always inferior to the other, as in this case, choosing a high price is the dominant strategy.

        v. The dominant strategy for each firm choosing a low price also happens to be an example of the *Prisoner's Dilemma* in this particular payoff matrix. If given the opportunity to work together, both firm A and B would likely agree to each set a high price and earn higher daily profits of $1000 rather than $750. But, because they are unable to collude, then they each must assume that the other player will choose the low-price strategy.

vi. A *Nash Equilibrium* exists when no player can increase their payoff in the game by individually choosing a different strategy. Looking back at the payoff matrix, you can see that neither player has an incentive to switch from their low-price strategy. Depending on the payoff matrix, it is possible to have no, one, or multiple Nash Equilibria in a game.

Test Tip

Firms don't always have a dominant strategy. In the payoff matrix below, notice that Firm A has a dominant strategy of setting a low price, but Firm B's strategy depends on Firm A's course of action and is thus not a dominant strategy. If Firm A sets a high price, then Firm B maximizes profit by setting a low price, but if Firm A sets a low price, then Firm B maximizes profit by setting a high price.

	Firm A High Price	Firm A Low Price
Firm B High Price	A: $1000 B: $1000	A: $1200 B: $ 800
Firm B Low Price	A: $ 500 B: $1200	A: $ 750 B: $ 750

This problem can still be solved in the sense that you can predict what each firm will do. Start with Firm A having a dominant strategy. Now Firm B, knowing this, should choose its best response to Firm A's dominant strategy because it is known what Firm A will do. So, in this case, Firm A chooses to price low and Firm B chooses to price high. Firm A yields $1200 and Firm B yields $800.

UNIT 5

FACTOR MARKETS

Factor Markets

I. **Topics 5.1 & 5.2: Introduction to Factor Markets and Changes in Factor Demand and Factor Supply**

A. *Factor markets* are the markets for the factors of production (land, labor, capital, and entrepreneurship).

B. Markets happen whenever consumers and producers meet to exchange goods, services, or in this case, factors of production.

Test Tip

The AP® Microeconomics exam focuses primarily on the markets for labor and capital.

You're likely to see questions that ask you to use the supply and demand concepts you already know to answer questions about the price and quantity of land, labor, capital, and entrepreneurship. For example, a decrease in the supply of skilled labor will have what effect on the wage rate and employment in the skilled labor market? Answer: A decrease in supply results in an increase in price (translation: increased wage rate) and a decrease in quantity (translation: decreased employment).

Application and translation of these concepts might sometimes be tricky, but usually can be made easier by keeping in mind that, in factor or resource markets, firms are the buyers on the demand side of the market and households are the sellers on the supply side of the market. However, the idea of using marginal analysis to determine the right quantity is still our focus. In these cases, we'll be comparing marginal revenue product with marginal factor cost.

C. *Derived factor demand* refers to the fact that the demand for goods and services in the product markets creates demand for the factors of production to produce these goods and services.

   1. For example, an increase in the demand for hamburgers and french fries leads to more demand for beef, potatoes, cooks, stoves, ovens, deep-fryers, restaurant buildings, and burger entrepreneurs. Less demand for burgers and fries leads to less demand for the factors of production used to make them.

D. From where does the demand for the factors of production come? Factor demand comes from multiplying the firm's marginal revenue by its marginal product.

E. Recall that marginal revenue is the additional revenue that comes from selling an additional unit of output $\left(\dfrac{\Delta TR}{\Delta Q}\right)$.

   1. For example, a company named Apricot Computers increases its sales of laptops from 100 to 101 units and its total revenue increases from $100,000 to $101,000. What is Apricot Computers' marginal revenue from selling its 101st laptop?

   Answer: $1,000. Why? Total revenue increased by $1,000 when the company sold the additional laptop.

F. Marginal product is the additional output or product generated by employing an additional input $\left(\dfrac{\Delta Q}{\Delta L}\right)$.

   1. For example, Apricot Computers employs 20 workers and is able to produce 100 computers. If adding an additional worker increases total product from 100 to 101, then what's the marginal product of the 21st worker?

   Answer: The marginal product of the 21st worker is one computer.

G. *Marginal revenue product* (MRP) is the change in total revenue generated when one additional input is employed $\left(\frac{\Delta TR}{\Delta L}\right)$. It decreases as additional workers are hired due to the principle of diminishing marginal returns.

1. Marginal Revenue Product is equal to marginal revenue multiplied by marginal product (MRP = MR × MP).

2. Using the example above, the MRP for Apricot Computers' 21st worker is $1,000.

3. For perfectly-competitive firms, where marginal revenue equals price, marginal revenue product can also be calculated by multiplying price by marginal product (MRP = P × MP).

4. Compared with perfectly-competitive (price-taking) firms, monopolistically-competitive firms, oligopolists, and monopolists generally have less MRP because marginal revenue for these firms is less than the price. It also slopes down faster because marginal product declines as firms hire additional workers *and* the value of each unit produced to the firm declines as they produce more and more.

5. MRP is factor demand, so increases in product prices, marginal revenue, or marginal product increase MRP and thus increase factor demand (i.e., demand for labor, demand for capital, etc.).

   ➤ Examples of causes of rightward shifts in MRP include worker-training programs, technological advances in production methods, increases in the popularity of the good produced, and so forth.

H. *Marginal-factor cost* (MFC) is the extra cost a firm incurs when employing one additional unit of input such as a worker or machine $\left(\frac{\Delta TC}{\Delta L} \text{ or } \frac{\Delta TC}{\Delta K}\right)$.

I. In perfectly-competitive factor markets, MFC is equal to either the wage rate (labor market) or rental rate (capital market).

J. Just as the product markets can be arranged on a spectrum from perfectly-competitive to monopolistic, factor markets can have different structures. Perfectly-competitive factor markets are those in which a large number of firms are acting to hire similar workers. Each firm's hiring decisions cannot affect the market wage rate because each firm is hiring only a very small percentage of the industry quantity. Such firms are referred to as *wage takers.*

K. The following side-by-side graphs (Figure 10.1) illustrate a perfectly-competitive market for labor (a type of factor market) and how that market appears to a perfectly-competitive firm.

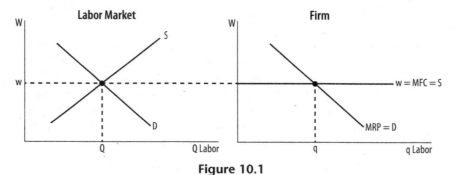

Figure 10.1

L. The market wage (w) is determined by the equilibrium of the supply and demand for labor in the graph on the left. The market labor demand curve is the total of all the firms' MRP curves and the market-supply curve is determined by the labor force's willingness to hire more labor at higher wage rates.

M. In a competitive market, firms such as the one depicted in the graph on the right are able to employ as much labor at the market wage as they are willing to hire (wage takers face a horizontal or perfectly elastic supply curve—they can choose any quantity and the price is constant).

N. For the firm in the graph on the right, the market wage (w) is the firm's marginal factor cost (MFC) and the supply (S) it faces. Supply equals marginal factor cost because wage is constant.

O. Firms hire the quantity of labor (q) that corresponds to the intersection of the firm's marginal revenue product (MRP) curve, which is also its demand for labor and the firm's MFC, which is also the supply curve it faces.

P. Note the similarity between this set of side-by-side graphs (Figure 10.2) and those for perfectly-competitive product markets. Though the graphs have many likenesses, the differences are just as important:

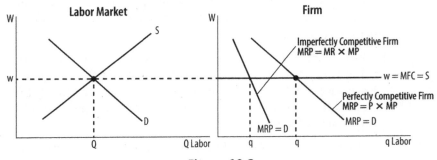

Figure 10.2

1. Labels (wage rather than price, quantity of labor rather than quantity of output, MRP rather than MR, MFC rather than MC)

2. Supply rather than demand is horizontal for the firm (difference between a price taker and a wage taker)

Actors have different roles. When answering AP® test questions about manipulation of these labor markets, remember that words that make you think about the willingness of workers would influence supply because individuals selling their labor are suppliers in these markets. Words that make you think about firms and their interest in hiring would influence demand because firms are the buyers in these markets.

Q. Imperfectly-competitive firms will employ less labor than perfectly-competitive firms given the same MFC because their MRP (MR × MP) is less than the perfectly-competitive firm's MRP (P × MP). The reason for this is that MR < P for any firm that is not perfectly competitive (i.e., monopoly, oligopoly, and monopolistic competition).

II. Topic 5.3: Profit-Maximizing Behavior in Perfectly Competitive Factor Markets

A. Firms try to make as much profit as possible. One way they can reach this goal is by decreasing their costs without decreasing their output. This means that they need to find the right mix of labor (workers) and capital (machines) to achieve productive efficiency (lowest ATC).

1. Firms can find the combination of labor (L) and capital (k) that is least costly by following this rule: set the marginal product of labor (MPL) divided by the price of labor (PL) equal to the marginal product of capital (MPk) divided by the price of capital (Pk).

2. The rule can be abbreviated in either of the following ways:

$$\frac{MPL}{PL} = \frac{MPk}{Pk}$$

$$\frac{MPL}{MPk} = \frac{PL}{Pk}$$

3. Remember that the MPL and MPk decrease as firms increase the use of labor and capital. So if $\frac{MPL}{PL} > \frac{MPk}{Pk}$, the firm should employ more labor and use less capital to minimize its ATC. If, on the other hand, $\frac{MPL}{PL} < \frac{MPk}{Pk}$, the firm should employ less labor and employ more capital in order to minimize its ATC.

For example, assume MPL = 10, PL = $5, MPK = 20, and PK = $4. Given the numbers above, what should the firm do with its use of labor and capital to minimize its average total cost?

$$\frac{MPL}{PL} < \frac{MPK}{PK} \text{ because } \frac{10}{\$5} < \frac{20}{\$4}$$

In this case, the firm should employ more capital or less labor to minimize its cost.

The math and thinking behind the cost-minimizing input combination and the utility-maximizing rule are very similar. Once you know how to do one of them, you can easily solve both types of problems.

III. Topic 5.4: Monopsonistic Markets

A. *Monopsony* occurs when there is only one consumer in a market.

B. If there is monopsony in the factor market, this means there is only one employer of labor and/or capital. A town with one large factory that is the only employer of significant numbers of workers who don't have specialized skills is a good approximation of a monopsony.

C. Monopsony in the factor market leads to marginal factor cost increasing at a faster rate than the labor supply curve because as more factors are employed, the price of the last unit employed must be paid to all of the previous units as well. In other words, the assumption is made that monopsonists cannot wage discriminate. For example, as a monoposonist firm attempts to hire more labor, it must not only offer a higher wage to the prospective workers, but it must also pay that wage to the workers already employed.

D. The result of monopsony in the factor market is a lower price for the factors of production (wages, rents), and a lower quantity of factors employed.

E. The following graph (Figure 10.3) illustrates the difference in outcomes between monopsony and perfect competition in the factor market. The monopsony wage (w) is lower than the competitive wage (w′). The monopsony quantity (Q) is less than the competitive quantity (Q).

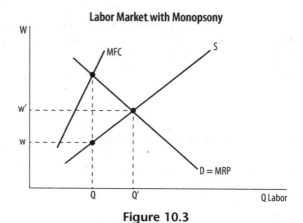

Labor Market with Monopsony

Figure 10.3

> *Although monopsony has not shown up often on the free-response section of the exam, many students and teachers were surprised when it did show up on a previous AP® Microeconomics Form B exam. It is worth your time to be able to both draw and understand monopsony.*

Test Tip

UNIT 6

MARKET FAILURE AND THE ROLE OF GOVERNMENT

Market Failure and the Role of Government

Topic 6.1: Socially Efficient and Inefficient Market Outcomes

A. *Social efficiency* is achieved when the marginal social benefit (MSB) of consuming a good or service is equal to the marginal social cost (MSC) of producing the good or service. This means that all of the costs of production and all of the benefits of consumption are internalized in the equilibrium price and quantity. MSB = MSC means that the optimal level of output is achieved where the cost to society of producing the last unit is equal to the benefit society derives from its consumption. Any more output would result in the cost exceeding the benefit. Any less output would result in a potential welfare gain for society.

    1. Social efficiency maximizes economic welfare as seen in Figure 11.1. The sum of producer and consumer surplus equals total economic surplus.

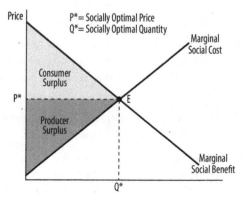

Figure 11.1

2. P* represents the socially optimal price and Q* represents the socially optimal quantity.

3. In perfectly competitive markets, the supply curve equals the marginal social cost curve and the demand curve equals the marginal social benefit curve, only if all social benefits and costs are internalized by individuals in the market.

B. Imperfectly competitive markets, such as monopoly, oligopoly, and monopolistic competition result in equilibrium price and quantity outcomes that are less than socially optimal or efficient.

C. *Market failures* happen when a market does not allocate or distribute goods or services efficiently, or when markets fail to provide certain goods or services.

It's not uncommon for a free-response question to test your understanding of multiple topic areas at the same time. For example, a question about monopolistic competition might also test your understanding of market failures. Be able to adapt your understanding of one topic to other topic areas.

II. Topic 6.2: Externalities

A. *Externalities* are unintended side effects of the production and consumption of a good or service.

1. Sometimes a good or service creates a benefit for some that are neither the producer nor the consumer of the good or service. When this happens, economists call it a *positive externality*.

   i. An example of a good that provides a positive externality is the flu vaccine.

   ii. When doctors and nurses (producers) "give" (sell) flu shots to their patients (consumers), both the producers and the consumers benefit. Other people who have not consumed the flu vaccine still receive benefits because as more people pay to get flu shots, the risk of the flu goes down not only for the consumers, but also for those who did not pay to get the shot. Similarly, buying and planting flowers in one's yard not only benefits the gardener—neighbors may enjoy the view or benefit from increased interest if selling a home.

iii. If a good or service creates a positive externality, then its marginal benefit to society, or *marginal social benefit (MSB)* is greater than its marginal benefit to just the consumers, or *marginal private benefit (MPB)*. Marginal private benefit is the market demand and in this case understates the true benefit the product provides.

iv. The following graph (Figure 11.2) shows the market for flu vaccine that creates a positive externality. The presence of a positive externality creates deadweight loss because the private market for the vaccine does not produce the allocatively efficient quantity at the market equilibrium, MSB > MC, indicating an underproduction of the good. Notice the difference between the market equilibrium price (p) and quantity (q) and the *socially optimal* price (p*) and quantity (q*). The socially optimal price (p*) and quantity (q*) are allocatively efficient because the MSB = MC.

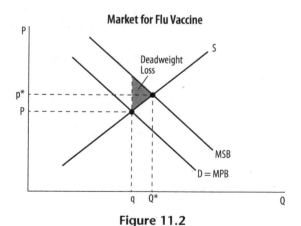

Market for Flu Vaccine

Figure 11.2

2. Many forms of production create some *negative externality*. A negative externality happens when somebody other than

the producer or consumer is forced to bear some of the costs of production.

i. An example of negative externality is air pollution. Many power plants burn coal in order to produce electricity—and this creates air pollution. Others who neither produce nor consume the electricity are left with costs such as damages from acid rain, medical bills from asthma treatment, and so on.

ii. If a good or service creates a negative externality, then its marginal cost to society, or *marginal social cost (MSC)* is greater than its marginal cost to just the producer, or *marginal private cost (MPC)*. Marginal private cost is the market supply, which in these situations understates the true cost of making the product in question.

iii. The following graph (Figure 11.3) shows the market for electricity which creates a negative externality, pollution. The presence of a negative externality creates deadweight loss because the private market for electricity does not produce the allocatively efficient quantity at the market equilibrium MSC > MB, indicating overproduction. Notice the difference between the market equilibrium price (p) and quantity (q) and the socially optimal price (p*) and quantity (q*). The socially optimal price (p*) and quantity (q*) are allocatively efficient because the MSC = MB.

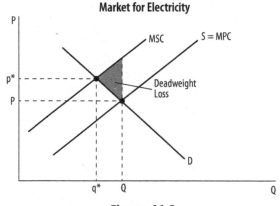

Market for Electricity

Figure 11.3

3. Remedies for externalities often come from the government.

   i.   In the case of a positive externality, the government can provide a per-unit *subsidy* to either the producer or consumer in order to achieve the socially optimal quantity of output.

   ii. The following graphs (Figure 11.4) show how a per-unit subsidy paid to the consumer of flu vaccine would affect the market. Notice that the subsidy increases the demand for the vaccine so that the MPB = MSB and allocative efficiency in the market is achieved.

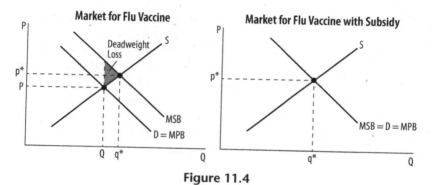

Figure 11.4

   iii. In the case of negative externalities, government can assess a per-unit tax on producers in order to bring about the socially optimal price and quantity.

   iv. The graphs in Figure 11.5 show how a per-unit tax on the producer of electricity would affect the market. Notice that the tax raises the marginal private cost at every level of output (acting as a decrease in supply) of producing electricity so that the MPC = MSC and allocative efficiency in the market is again achieved.

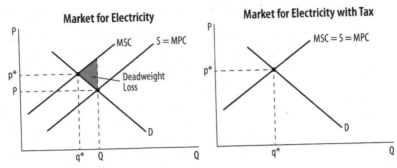

Figure 11.5

v. The *Coase Theorem* says that an allocatively efficient outcome can be reached without government involvement. If the cost of bargaining is zero and private-property rights are clearly defined, then (in the case of a negative externality) the producer and the party victim can negotiate a payment to address the externality. Either the victim can pay the producer to not produce, or the producer can pay the victim so as to offset the cost of the externality.

III. Topic 6.3: Public and Private Goods

A. Most goods and services are provided through markets, but sometimes markets fail to provide a necessary good or service. It is then up to the government to provide these public goods.

1. What makes some goods suitable to being produced by the government and paid for by tax money rather than being allocated in the private market?

   i. Public goods are typically *non-rival* and *non-excludable.* Examples include police protection, national defense, and most bridges and public highways.

   ii. Private goods can be *rival* or non-rival, but they are always excludable. Examples include candy bars, concerts, haircuts, cars, and houses. Sometimes government may choose to produce private goods to allow free access to those who cannot pay.

iii. A good or service is rival if one person's consumption prevents another person from consuming that unit of the good or service.

> ➤ For example, if Shauna and Marco both have a headache, Shauna's consumption of an aspirin means that Marco can't take that same pill. He can take another pill from the same bottle, but once Shauna has consumed her pill, Marco can't consume the same pill. The same is true for most goods, such as hamburgers, gallons of gasoline, and shoes.

iv. A good or service is non-rival if one person's consumption does not diminish the ability of another person to consume the same good or service.

> ➤ Jim and Sarah can simultaneously consume the same movie at a theater. When some people cross a bridge or walk through a park, it doesn't prevent other people from crossing that bridge or walking through the same park.

v. A good or service is excludable if it can be withheld from those who are either unable or unwilling to pay.

> ➤ Jim's and Sarah's movie is excludable. If they didn't buy a ticket, they would not have been able to watch the movie at the theater. Likewise, restaurants can decide not to serve food to those who don't pay and museums can deny entrance to those who refuse to buy a ticket.

vi. A good or service is non-excludable if it cannot be withheld from those unwilling or unable to pay.

> ➤ Police protection is an example of a service provided to all consumers regardless of their willingness or ability to pay for the service. Another example of a non-excludable good or service is a storm-siren that warns a city of a tornado. Whether you pay for it or not, you'll still hear the siren.

IV. Topic 6.4: The Effects of Government Intervention in Different Market Structures

A. Imperfectly competitive markets such as monopolistic competition, oligopoly, and monopoly are examples of market failures. They do not provide the socially optimal price and quantity of a good or service.

1. The government either breaks up or regulates some imperfectly-competitive firms such as monopolies in order to promote competition and efficiency.

2. In the following graphs (Figures 11.6, 11.7, and 11.8) compare the differences between the unregulated and the regulated natural monopoly.

3. Figure 11.6 illustrates an unregulated natural monopoly. The unregulated natural monopoly produces less output at a higher price than it would if it were regulated for either productive efficiency (P = ATC) or allocative efficiency (P = MC).

4. Figure 11.7 illustrates a natural monopoly regulated to produce at a productively efficient quantity and price. The result is a higher quantity and lower price than the unregulated natural monopoly seen in Figure 11.6. However, deadweight loss still exists because the price is greater than the marginal cost.

5. If the government wants the natural monopoly to produce at the allocatively efficient quantity, then they will set the price equal to the marginal cost and provide a lump-sum subsidy to offset the firm's losses as seen in Figure 11.8.

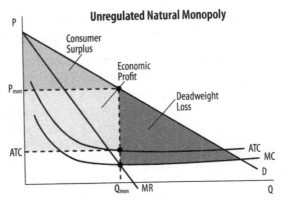

Figure 11.6

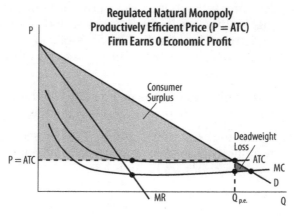

Figure 11.7

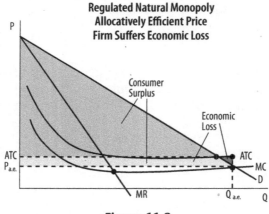

Figure 11.8

Topic 6.5: Inequality

A. Equity

1. Markets fail to allocate income equally. Some households earn more income while others earn less.

2. Differences in worker productivity, changing trade patterns, past discrimination, and tax policies are some of the reasons

for differences in incomes between households. For example, an increase in demand for skilled labor and a decrease in demand for unskilled labor results in less income equality as skilled workers' incomes rise and unskilled workers' incomes fall.

3. Two measures of income equality are the *Lorenz Curve* and the *Gini Coefficient*.

4. The Lorenz Curve is a graph of income inequality that shows the percentage of a country's income earned by a percentage of a country's households.

Test Tip *You should know and understand the Lorenz Curve and the Gini Coefficient. However, you will not be required to draw the Lorenz Curve or calculate the Gini Coefficient on the AP® Microeconomics exam.*

5. In Figure 11.9, the 45-degree line represents perfect income equality. The bowed-out line is the Lorenz Curve for the country and shows the distribution of income.

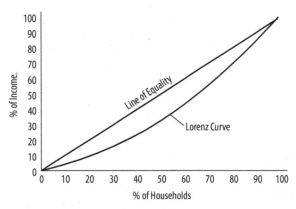

Figure 11.9

6. Look at the following graph (Figure 11.10). Point A shows that 50 percent of the households earn only 33 percent of the income, which also means that the top half of house-

holds earn two-thirds of the nation's income. Point B shows that 88 percent of the households earn 80 percent of the income, meaning that the richest 12 percent of households earn one-fifth of the income in the society.

Figure 11.10

7. In the following graph (Figure 11.11), the Lorenz Curve is further away from the line of equality. This means that income is less evenly allocated in the country than in the previous graph.

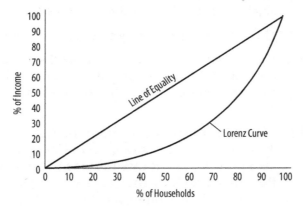

Figure 11.11

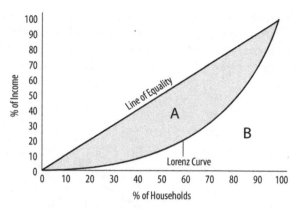

Figure 11.12

8. A related measure of income inequality is the *Gini Coefficient*. The Gini Coefficient compares the area between the line of equality and a Lorenz curve with the total area under the line of equality.

9. In the previous graph (Figure 11.12), the Gini Coefficient is equal to area A divided by the sum of areas A and B. Gini Coefficient $= \dfrac{A}{A + B}$. Because area A + B is equal to half (axes range from 0 to 100 percent which is 1), 2A is also an algebraic equivalent for the Gini Coefficient.

10. The Gini Coefficient ranges from zero to one.

11. A Gini Coefficient of zero means perfect income equality. Every household earns an equal amount of income, and the society's Lorenz Curve is the line of equality. Area A equals zero.

12. A Gini Coefficient of one means perfect income inequality. One household earns all of the income while the rest earn nothing. In this case the area B is zero, which means that the society's Lorenz Curve follows the x-axis until 100 percent and then jumps vertically upward to the point (100 percent, 100 percent).

13. In the real world, Gini Coefficients fall somewhere in between the two extremes. Gini Coefficients closer to zero mean income is more equally distributed, while Gini Coef-

ficients closer to one mean that the income distribution is more unequal.

B. Tax Progressivity

1. Economists classify taxes according to how they reallocate income in an economy.

   i. *Progressive taxes* are those taxes that take a higher percentage of the income of high-income earners than from low-income earners. The effect of progressive taxes is to make the income distribution more equal. An example of a progressive tax is the federal income tax (at least in theory). Other examples include the *estate tax* and *gift taxes*.

Test Tip

With a topic such as tax progressivity, it might be tempting to express your political viewpoint on taxes. Doing this on the exam is a waste of time because opinions are not graded. Only microeconomic analysis earns you points on the exam.

   ii. *Regressive taxes* are those that take a lower percentage of the income of high-income earners than of low-income earners. The effect of regressive taxes is to make the income distribution less equal. Sales tax is an example of a regressive tax because high-income earners pay tax only on the income they spend, and they save more than low-income earners.

   iii. *Proportional taxes* place an equal burden on all household income levels and should not affect the distribution of income. A flat-rate tax on income or a tithe are examples of proportional taxes.

C. Principles of Taxation

1. The *ability to pay* principle of taxation says that taxes should be collected from those with enough income to pay the tax. In the United States, the Federal income tax is an example of taxation according to the ability-to-pay principle. Those with higher incomes pay the tax while those with low incomes pay very little of the tax, or even none at all.

2. The *benefit* principle of taxation says that those who benefit from a public good or service should pay the tax for the good or service. For example, taxes on gasoline that go to pay for road construction, maintenance, and improvement are based on the benefit principle.

Students should be familiar with how taxes affect a firm's costs of production. Lump-sum taxes are a fixed cost and as such only affect AFC and ATC. Per-unit taxes are a variable cost and thus affect VC and MC. For example, a per-unit tax affects not only a firm's cost of production, but affects the profit-maximizing quantity of output because of its effect on MC. Lump-sum taxes, however, only affect fixed costs so they have no effect on the firm's profit-maximizing quantity of output.

PART III

KEY GRAPHS AND FORMULAS

Key Graphs

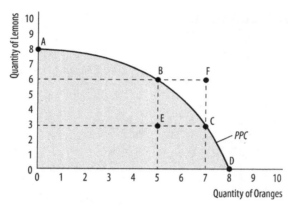

Figure 12.1

I. The Production Possibilities Curve (PPC)

A. The PPC shows all of the possible combinations of two goods that can be produced if the factors of production are used efficiently, that is, with the least amount of waste. The only thing that changes in the model is the production combination. The amount of resources, time, and technology do not change in the model. If these things *do* change, the model changes.

B. In the graph above, points A, B, C, and D are productively efficient because they lie on the curve.

C. Point E, which lies below the curve, is productively inefficient because resources are not being fully employed.

D. Point F, which lies above the curve, is unattainable given the current technology and resources. Economic growth can shift the PPC outward so that previously unattainable points become possible choices for a society.

E. The reason for the PPC's convex shape (bowed outward) is the *law of increasing opportunity cost*. A PPC that is a straight line reflects constant opportunity cost.

II. Supply and Demand

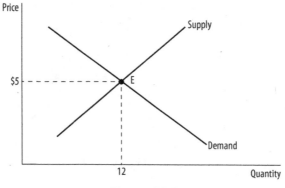

Figure 12.2

A. Supply and demand models the behavior of a competitive market. *Market equilibrium* occurs when quantity supplied equals quantity demanded and results in the equilibrium price and quantity traded.

B. Changes in market size, expectations, related prices, income, and tastes result in a shift in demand and thus equilibrium.

   1. Increased demand (shift right) results in a higher price and quantity.

   2. Decreased demand (shift left) results in a lower price and quantity.

C. Changes in technology, related production, input prices, and expectations result in a shift in supply and thus equilibrium.

    1. Increased supply (right shift) results in a lower price but higher quantity.

    2. Decreased supply (left shift) results in a higher price but lower quantity.

III. Price Ceilings

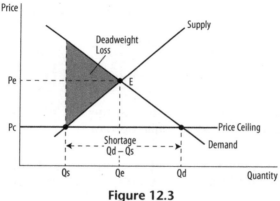

Figure 12.3

A. *Price ceilings* (Pc) are legal maximum prices.

B. Price ceilings are effective (that is, they go into effect) if they are set below the market equilibrium price (Pe).

C. Effective price ceilings result in a shortage equal to the quantity demanded (Qd) minus the quantity supplied (Qs).

D. Effective price ceilings result in deadweight loss because marginal benefit (MB) costs are greater than the marginal costs (MC) at the quantity supplied (Qs) (MB > MC at Qs). Only Qs units are traded, and Qe is the allocatively efficient quantity.

IV. Price Floors

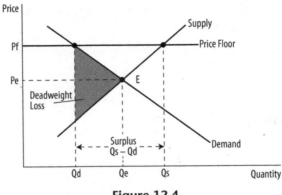

Figure 12.4

A. *Price floors* (Pf) are legal minimum prices.

B. Price floors are effective (that is, they go into effect) if they are set above the market equilibrium price.

C. Effective price floors result in a surplus equal to the quantity supplied (Qs) minus the quantity demanded (Qd).

D. Effective price floors result in deadweight loss because P > MC at Qd. Only Qd units are traded, and Qe is the allocatively efficient quantity.

V. **Production Function**

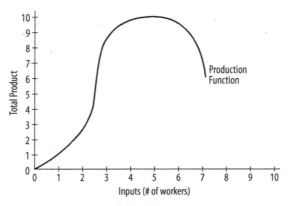

Figure 12.5

A. In the graph above, the production function shows how a firm's product (output) changes as one input (usually labor) is varied.

B. At first, total product and marginal product increases as inputs are added. This stage of production is called *increasing-marginal returns.*

C. The production function shows that as further inputs are added, total product increases but marginal product decreases. This stage of production is called *diminishing-marginal returns.*

D. Finally, the production function shows that adding even more inputs results in both total product and the marginal product decreasing; that is, marginal product is negative. This stage of production is called *decreasing returns.*

VI. Per-Unit Cost Curves

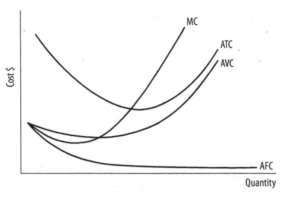

Figure 12.6

A. MC is *marginal cost*. MC = the change in total cost divided by the change in quantity. MC is the cost of producing an additional unit of output. Marginal cost bears a very close relationship with supply.

B. ATC is *average total cost*. ATC = total cost divided by quantity. Productive efficiency is achieved when a firm produces output at the minimum of average total cost. ATC is also the total of the two curves (AVC and AFC).

C. AVC is *average variable cost*. AVC = variable cost divided by quantity. The minimum of AVC is the shut-down point for firms.

D. AFC is *average fixed cost*. AFC = fixed cost divided by quantity. AFC decreases quickly as a firm's output increases. AFC is often absent from this graph but can be inferred because it is the space between ATC and AVC.

VII. Perfect Competition

A. *Perfect competition* has two graphs. The first is the market and the second is the firm.

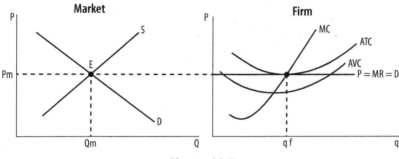

Figure 12.7

B. The price comes from the market equilibrium. Being a *price taker*, the firm takes the market price as its price, demand, and marginal revenue curves (MR). These are perfectly elastic and horizontal.

C. The firm produces the quantity associated with MR = MC.

D. In the long run, the firm makes zero economic profit as it produces where P = ATC's minimum.

E. The firm can earn short-run economic profits when P > ATC.

F. The firm will choose to operate at a loss if ATC > P > AVC.

G. The firm will shut down and q = 0 when P < AVC.

H. Perfect competition is productively efficient in the long run because q is at minimum ATC.

I. Perfect competition is always allocatively efficient because P = MC no matter whether the firm is taking a loss, making a profit, or breaking even in long-run equilibrium.

VIII. Monopoly

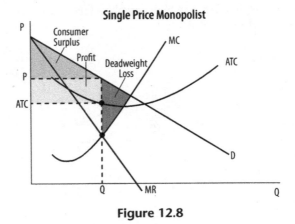

Figure 12.8

A. The firm produces the profit-maximizing quantity associated with MR = MC.

B. The monopoly firm makes economic profit when it produces when P > ATC.

C. Monopoly oftentimes is not productively efficient because Q is not always at minimum ATC.

D. Monopoly is *not* allocatively efficient because P > MC, resulting in deadweight loss.

E. If a monopolist can perfectly price discriminate, then consumer surplus becomes profit, and Q increases to become allocatively efficient because MR shifts to become demand.

IX. Monopolistic Competition

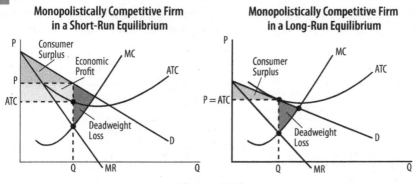

Figure 12.9

A. The firm produces the profit-maximizing quantity associated with MR = MC.

B. The *monopolistically-competitive firm* makes economic profit in the short run if it produces when P > ATC.

C. Monopolistic competition is *not* productively efficient in the long run because Q is *not* at minimum ATC. Monopolistic competition results in excess capacity because the firm produces less output than it could at lowest ATC.

D. Monopolistic competition is *not* allocatively efficient because P > MC, resulting in deadweight loss.

E. In the long run, economic profits attract competition that reduces demand and results in zero economic profit. If the firm had been taking a loss in the short run, firms would leave the industry, increasing demand to the same zero economic profit situation shown in the graph above on the right.

X. Oligopoly

A. Firms behave interdependently in *oligopoly*. They make their own price and production decisions, but carefully consider the price and production decisions their competition might make as well.

B. A payoff matrix shows the combination of outcomes for two firms.

	Firm A High Price	Firm A Low Price
Firm B **High Price**	A: $1000 B: $1000	A: $1200 B: $ 500
Firm B **Low Price**	A: $ 500 B: $1200	A: $ 750 B: $ 750

C. In oligopoly, firms sometimes have an incentive to collude and not compete. Often theses collusive arrangements are short-lived due to the incentive for some firms to cheat.

D. When a firm's pricing/production strategy does not depend on the decision of its competitor, it's a dominant strategy and the inferior choice is called a *dominated strategy*.

E. When a firm's pricing/production strategy is dependent on the decision of its competitor, it is *non-dominant*.

F. A Nash Equilibrium exists in the payoff matrix when neither player has an incentive to change their strategy.

XI. Competitive Factor Market

A. A *competitive factor market* exists when individual firms do not influence the marginal factor cost (MFC). In other words, they behave as wage takers.

B. The market wage becomes their supply and marginal factor cost curves.

C. Changes in the equilibrium factor price result in a change in the firm's factor supply.

D. The firm's demand for a factor of production is equal to the marginal revenue product (MRP) of the factor.

E. Firms that face perfect competition in the product market have an $MRP = P \times MP$.

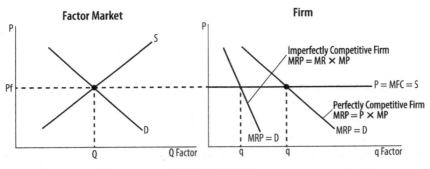

Figure 12.10

F. All firms' MRP may be calculated as change in total revenue divided by change in number of units of the input.

G. MRP and thus factor demand are greater for perfectly-competitive firms than for imperfectly competitive firms, so perfectly competitive firms will employ more factors of production (land, labor, capital, and entrepreneurship).

H. All firms maximize profits by employing the quantity of factors determined by $MFC = MRP$.

XII. Monopsonistic Markets

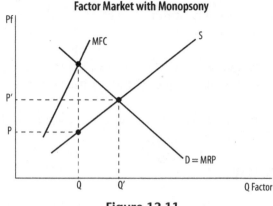

Factor Market with Monopsony

Figure 12.11

A. *Monopsony* in a factor market occurs when only one firm acts as a consumer. This fact gives the firm market power and as a result it behaves as a wage maker.

B. The marginal factor cost increases faster than the factor price because as the firm seeks to employ more units of a factor, the price offered by the firm applies to all of the units employed and not just to the last one employed.

C. The firm maximizes profit by employing the quantity of factors determined by MFC = MRP.

D. The factor price is determined by the intersection of profit-maximizing quantity and the factor supply curve.

E. Monopsony in the factor market results in a lower quantity of factor employment and a lower factor price than what occurs in competitive factor markets.

XIII. Positive Externality

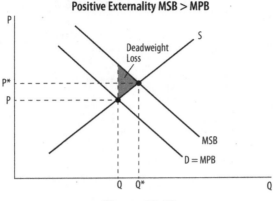

Figure 12.12

A. *Positive externality* exists when the marginal social benefit of a good or service exceeds the marginal private benefit (market demand) of a good or service. In simpler terms, a positive externality exists when the market price and quantity are too low.

B. The presence of a positive externality creates deadweight loss because allocative efficiency is not achieved by the market.

C. Government can remedy the deadweight loss of positive externality in the market by providing a per unit subsidy to consumers in order to achieve the allocatively efficient outcome (P*, Q*).

XIV. Negative Externality

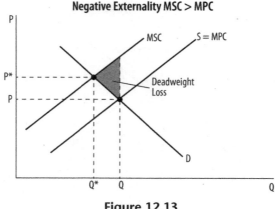

Figure 12.13

A. *Negative externality* exists when the marginal social cost (MSC) of a good or service exceeds the marginal private cost (market supply) of a good or service. In simpler terms, a negative externality exists when the market price is too low and the market quantity is too high.

B. The presence of a negative externality creates deadweight loss because allocative efficiency is not achieved by the market.

C. Government can remedy the deadweight loss of negative externality in the market by placing a per unit tax on producers in order to achieve the allocatively efficient outcome (P*, Q*). Other remedies for overproduction, such as price floors, price ceilings, and quotas (a limit on the number of units produced), may rectify the misallocation of goods.

XV. The Lorenz Curve

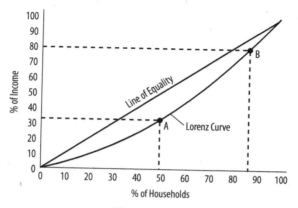

Figure 12.14

A. The *Lorenz Curve* is a graph of income inequality that shows the percentage of a country's income earned by a percentage of the country's households. *You will not be required to draw this graph on the AP® exam.*

B. Point A shows that 50 percent of the households earn only 33 percent of the income. Point B shows that 88 percent of the household earns 80 percent of the income.

C. The lower the Lorenz Curve sags below the 45-degree angle line of perfect equality, the more unevenly income is distributed.

Key Formulas

I. **Opportunity Cost**

A. Opportunity Cost of Producing Good y =
Amount of Good x Sacrificed per unit of Good y produced.

1. When measuring the amount of production, the opportunity cost of good $y = \dfrac{\text{units of } y \text{ made in a period of time}}{\text{units of } x \text{ made in a period of time}}$.

2. When measuring the amount of time it takes to produce, the opportunity cost of good $y = \dfrac{\text{hours to make an } x}{\text{hours to make an y}}$.

II. **Marginal Analysis**

A. If MB > MC, then produce and consume more to maximize benefit.

B. If MB < MC, then produce and consume less to maximize benefit.

C. If MB = MC, then total benefit is maximized.

III. **Equilibrium, Surpluses and Shortages**

A. If Qs = Qd, then market is in equilibrium.

B. If Qs > Qd, then surplus = Qs – Qd.

C. If Qs < Qd, then shortage = Qd – Qs.

Consumer Surplus, Producer Surplus, Deadweight Loss

 A. Consumer surplus is found below demand, above price paid, and to the left of quantity purchased.

 B. Producer surplus is found above supply (or marginal cost), below price received, and to the left of quantity sold.

 C. Deadweight loss is always found between quantity traded and the allocatively efficient quantity. It will appear below marginal benefit (demand) and above marginal cost (supply) if a good has been underproduced. It will appear above marginal benefit and below marginal cost if a good has been overproduced.

 D. Area of a triangle $= \dfrac{\text{base} \times \text{height}}{2}$.

V. **Total Revenue = P × Q.**

 Elasticity Formulas

 A. Price Elasticity of Demand (Ed)

  1. $\text{Ed} = \dfrac{\% \text{ change in Qd}}{\% \text{ change in P}}$.

  2. If Ed > 1, then elastic.

  3. If Ed = 1, then unit elastic.

  4. If Ed < 1, then inelastic.

  5. If Ed = 0, then perfectly inelastic.

  6. If Ed is undefined, then perfectly elastic.

B. Income Elasticity of Demand (Ei)

1. $Ei = \dfrac{\% \text{ change in Qd}}{\% \text{ change in income}}$.

2. If Ei > 1, then normal luxury.

3. If 0 < Ei < 1, then normal necessity.

4. If Ei < 0, then inferior.

C. Cross-Price Elasticity of Demand (Exy)

1. $Exy = \dfrac{\% \text{ change in Qd of good } x}{\% \text{ change in P of good } y}$.

2. If Exy > 0, then substitute.

3. If Exy = 0, then unrelated.

4. If Exy < 0, then complement.

D. Elasticity of Supply (Es)

1. $Es = \dfrac{\% \text{ change in Qs}}{\% \text{ change in P}}$.

2. If Es > 1, then elastic.

3. If Es < 1, then inelastic.

4. If Es = 1 then unit is elastic.

VII. Utility Maximization Rule

A. Utility is maximized when $\dfrac{MUx}{Px} = \dfrac{MUy}{Py}$ or $\dfrac{MUx}{MUy} = \dfrac{Px}{Py}$.

B. If $\dfrac{MUx}{Px} > \dfrac{MUy}{Py}$, then consume more of x and less of y; as you do, MUx will decline and MUy will increase.

C. If $\dfrac{MUx}{Px} < \dfrac{MUy}{Py}$, then consume less of x and more of y; as you do, MUy will decline and MUx will increase.

VIII. **Production Formulas**

A. Average Product = $\dfrac{\text{Total Product}}{\text{\# of Inputs}}$.

B. Marginal (Physical) Product = $\dfrac{\text{Change in Total Product}}{\text{Change in Total Inputs}}$.

IX. **Cost Formulas**

A. $FC = AFC \times Q = TC - VC$.

B. $VC = AVC \times Q = TC - FC$.

C. $TC = ATC \times Q = FC + VC$.

D. $MC = \dfrac{\text{Change in Total Cost}}{\text{Change in Q}}$.

E. $AFC = \dfrac{FC}{Q} = ATC - AVC$.

F. $AVC = \dfrac{VC}{Q} = ATC - AFC$.

G. $ATC = \dfrac{TC}{Q} = AFC + AVC$.

X. **Cost Minimizing Input Combination**

A. Costs are minimized when $\dfrac{MRP_L}{P_L} = \dfrac{MRP_K}{P_K}$ or $\dfrac{MRP_L}{MRP_K} = \dfrac{P_L}{P_K}$.

B. If $\dfrac{MRP_L}{P_L} > \dfrac{MRP_K}{P_K}$, then the firm should employ more labor and less capital.

C. If $\dfrac{MRP_L}{P_L} < \dfrac{MRP_K}{P_K}$, then the firm should employ less labor and more capital.

XI. Profit

A. Accounting Profit = Total Revenue − Explicit Costs.

B. Economic Profit = Total Revenue − (Explicit Costs + Opportunity or Implicit Cost).

C. $MR = \dfrac{\text{Change in Total Revenue}}{\text{Change in Q}}$.

D. If MR = MC, then profit is maximized.

XII. Efficiency

A. If P = MC or MSC, then Allocative Efficiency; no deadweight loss.

B. If Q minimizes ATC, then Productive Efficiency.

XIII. Factor Market Formulas

A. Factor Demand = MRP = $\dfrac{\Delta TR}{\Delta L}$, and in the case of perfectly competitive firms, P × MPP.

B. When firms hire the quantity of factors associated with MRP = MFC, they maximize profit.

XIV. Market Failure Formulas

A. If MSB > MPB, then positive externality.

B. If MSC > MPC, then negative externality.

PART IV

TEST-TAKING STRATEGIES AND PRACTICE QUESTIONS

Mastering the Multiple-Choice Questions

The AP® Microeconomics exam's multiple-choice section is made up of 60 questions. You have 70 minutes to answer them. This means that on average you have one minute and ten seconds to answer each question. Time management is important!

I. Think Like an Economist

A. Don't waste time. All questions are of equal value, so if you're spending too much time on one question, then you have less time for other questions that are equally valuable.

B. *Never* skip a question.

   1. No points can possibly be earned for a skipped question.

   2. There is no penalty for wrong answers. There are only points for right answers.

C. How much is too much time? Two minutes is too much time. If you're stuck on a question for two minutes, just give it your best guess and move on!

D. When a question asks you about what happened to price and quantity, *graph it*! This makes hard questions easier and easy questions a snap.

E. Once you've completed the multiple-choice section, go back over the questions that you answered quickly.

1. Don't waste time going back over questions that you didn't understand.

2. For the questions that you understood, check that you didn't get tricked by a distractor choice.

F. If time still remains, take a mental snapshot of any graphs that are provided in the multiple-choice section. You might need to reproduce those graphs in the free-response section. It is also possible that something in a graph for one problem will jog your memory to help you get a different question right.

G. Use the process of elimination. This increases your odds quite a bit. You can almost always rule out at least one choice even if you feel stumped.

H. If answers are too alike, they can't both be right, so be wary of picking one or the other. If there are two answers that are opposites, it is often the case that one of those two is the correct choice.

Test Tip

Go into the test confidently. You read this book. You know what to expect. Relax, smile, and realize that for every question, you most likely have the right answer.

II. Question Types on the AP® Microeconomics Exam

A. First, it's important to understand that certain questions, with which you may be familiar from your classroom studies, don't appear on the AP® exam. The AP® Microeconomics exam does not use matching, fill-in-the-blank, or true-false questions. You also won't find "all of the above" or "none of the above" to choose as an answer choice.

B. There are four different kinds of multiple-choice questions that you will encounter on the exam:

1. **Defining and classifying questions** (they appear most frequently).

   i.   Know the AP® Microeconomics vocabulary. (See Chapter 2.)

   ii. Realize that even though some answer choices have accurate and factually correct information, they may not answer what the question is asking. It may be true, but is it relevant?

   Example:

   Producer surplus is defined as

   (A) opportunity cost plus total revenue

   (B) the difference between the price that producers would accept for a good and the price they earn

   (C) the difference between the resource costs and the price producers pay

   (D) total revenue minus variable cost

   (E) the product of external costs and benefits

   The correct answer is (B).

2. **Cause-and-effect questions.**

   i.   These questions might be a simple *if-then* type of question, so know how concepts are related to each other.

   ii. Some cause-and-effect questions may give you two, three, or even four columns of possible effects. You don't have to know every effect in order to get these types of questions correct. Focus on the columns you understand and eliminate the wrong answers. Often there is a chain of events that connect the order of the columns the test writers choose; this may help you figure your way through this type of question.

Example:

Assume that pecans and walnuts are substitute goods. An increase in the price of pecans will cause the price and quantity of walnuts to change in which of the following ways?

	Price	Quantity
(A)	No change	Increase
(B)	Decrease	Increase
(C)	Increase	Decrease
(D)	Decrease	Decrease
(E)	Increase	Increase

The correct answer is (E).

3. **Understanding a graph, chart, or equation questions.**

   i.   On a graph question, it helps to draw information on the graph that is given in the text of the question.

   ii. When given a chart of data, make sure that you pay attention to the headings. Sometimes not all of the information provided is necessary to solve the problem. Sometimes you need to take extra steps to manipulate the data that is given to turn it into a form you need. For example, you may need to use a total product column to create a marginal product column.

   iii. On equation questions, a general rule that will help you to answer most any microeconomics question is that setting MB, MSB, MR, MP or MRP equal to either MC, MSC, MP, or MFC usually maximizes profits or minimizes costs.

Example:

A firm seeking to minimize its average total cost for a given level of output will employ the quantities of labor and capital which result in

(A) MPL / PL > MPK / PK

(B) MPL / PL < MPK / PK

(C) MPL / MPK < PL / PK

(D) MPL / MPK = PL / PK

(E) MPL / MPK = PK / PL

The correct answer is (D).

4. **Math calculation questions** (these are infrequent).

i.   Simple arithmetic solves most of these kinds of questions, so there will be no need to use calculus or trigonometry. The test does not allow a calculator, and the test writers are not primarily testing your calculation skills, so they will be kind by giving you numbers that are relatively easy to work with. Use this to your advantage; if you think you need to do nasty, messy, and long calculations, then you have almost certainly set up the problem incorrectly.

Example:

If total product increases from 10 to 12 when a sixth worker is added to an assembly line, and total product increases from 12 to 13 when a seventh worker is added, then

(A) the marginal product of the seventh worker is 3

(B) the marginal product of the seventh worker is 2

(C) the marginal product of the sixth worker is 3

(D) the marginal product of the seventh worker is 1

(E) the marginal product of the seventh worker cannot be determined

The correct answer is (D).

III. General Tips

A. There will be easy questions and difficult questions. Some questions will feel very easy and you may wonder if they are intentional trick questions (usually they aren't). Some questions included in the test each year are answered correctly by one-third or fewer of the students taking the test. Do not let the hard questions discourage you. The best students will still miss questions, but they won't let poor performance on one tough question carry over into missing the next one.

B. Understand differences between short and long run and look for cues that tell you what thought process to use.

C. Know that you can miss a lot of questions and still do well. You can likely score a 5 while still missing about ten multiple-choice questions, which means you only need slightly more than 80 percent correct. You can likely score a 4 while still missing about 20 questions, which means you only need slightly more than 65 percent correct. Those projections assume you do equally well on the multiple-choice and free-response sections; often students come to the exam knowing that one of these two sections is a relative strength.

D. In the end, there are no substitutes for preparation and practice. But then, you knew that, which is why you are reading this book.

Practice Multiple-Choice Questions

Practice with the following AP®-style questions. Then go online to access our timed, full-length practice exam at *www.rea.com/studycenter.*

1. Members of a government planning committee meet once a month to set all of the industrial production targets and to determine all of the allocation for a nation's economic output. This type of decision making would most likely be found in which economic system?

    (A) Market economy

    (B) Mixed economy

    (C) Traditional economy

    (D) Free enterprise economy

    (E) Command economy

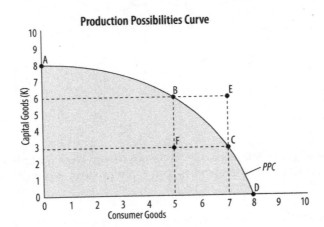

Production Possibilities Curve

2. Assume an economy is not fully employing all of
   its available resources. The decision to increase the
   production of capital goods is best illustrated by which
   of the following?

   (A) Moving from point B to point A with an opportunity
       cost of 5 consumer goods

   (B) Moving from point B to point E with an opportunity
       cost of 2 consumer goods

   (C) Moving from point F to point B with an opportunity
       cost of 0 consumer goods

   (D) Moving from point D to point C with an opportunity
       cost of 3 capital goods

   (E) Moving from point F to point C with an opportunity
       cost of 0 capital goods

3. Carlo and Bella decide to open a landscaping business. Assume that Carlo and Bella only have one spade for planting trees and a small hand-trowel for planting shrubs. Further assume Carlo is able to either plant 3 trees per hour or 18 shrubs per hour, while Bella is able to plant 4 trees per hour or 20 shrubs per hour. Which of the following statements best describes Carlo and Bella?

   (A) Carlo has a comparative advantage in planting trees and shrubs.

   (B) Carlo has a comparative advantage in planting trees, while Bella has an absolute advantage in planting trees.

   (C) Carlo and Bella both have a comparative advantage in planting shrubs.

   (D) Carlo has a comparative advantage in planting shrubs while Bella has a comparative advantage in planting trees.

   (E) Carlo has a comparative advantage in planting trees while Bella has an absolute advantage in planting shrubs.

4. Assume that a 10% increase in the price of good X results in both a 20% decrease in the quantity of good X demanded and a 15% increase in the quantity of good Y demanded. Which of the following is true?

   (A) Demand for good X is relatively inelastic and good Y is a complement to good X.

   (B) Demand for good X is relatively inelastic and good Y is a substitute for good X.

   (C) Demand for good X is relatively elastic and good Y is an unrelated good.

   (D) Demand for good X is relatively elastic and good Y is a substitute for good X.

   (E) Demand for good Y is relatively inelastic and good X is a perfect substitute for good Y.

5. Assume canned ham is an inferior good. Further assume the market for canned ham is perfectly competitive. An increase in consumers' incomes will most likely have what initial effect on the market for canned ham?

	Change in Supply	Change in Demand	Price	Quantity
(A)	Increase	No change	Decrease	Increase
(B)	Decrease	No change	Increase	Decrease
(C)	No change	Increase	Increase	Increase
(D)	No change	Decrease	Decrease	Decrease
(E)	Decrease	Increase	Decrease	Indeterminate

6. Assume the market for good X is perfectly competitive. Also assume the current price of good X results in a quantity supplied that is greater than the quantity demanded. For the market to achieve equilibrium, which of the following is most likely to take place?

    (A) Producers will increase the price of X and consumers will respond by buying less.

    (B) Producers will decrease the price of good X and consumers will respond by buying more.

    (C) Government will set an effective price floor.

    (D) Government will set an effective price ceiling.

    (E) Consumers will purchase a substitute for good X with a relatively higher price and demand less of good X.

7. Assume there is a market for a normal good with an effective price floor. Assuming the current price equals the effective price floor, an increase in per unit labor productivity will most likely result in which of the following?

   (A) Increased demand for the good and an increase in the price of the good

   (B) Decreased demand for the good and no change in the price of the good

   (C) Increased supply of the good and no change in the price of the good

   (D) Decreased supply of the good and no change in the price of the good

   (E) Increased demand for the good and no change in the price of the good

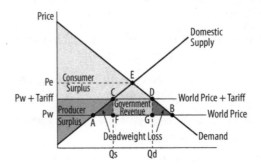

8. Removal of the tariff for the domestic market for a good will most likely result in which of the following?

	Consumer Surplus	Producer Surplus	Deadweight Loss	Quantity Imported
(A)	Increase	Decrease	Increase	Decrease
(B)	Increase	Decrease	Decrease	Decrease
(C)	Increase	Decrease	Decrease	Increase
(D)	Decrease	Increase	Increase	Increase
(E)	Decrease	Increase	Decrease	Increase

Number of workers	Total quantity of good Z produced
1	3
2	7
3	12
4	15
5	13

9. Use the production function from the chart. The point of diminishing marginal returns is reached with the addition of which worker?

(A) First worker

(B) Second worker

(C) Third worker

(D) Fourth worker

(E) Fifth worker

10. Which of the following best explains why the distance between curve (B) and curve (C) in the diagram below decreases as the quantity produced increases?

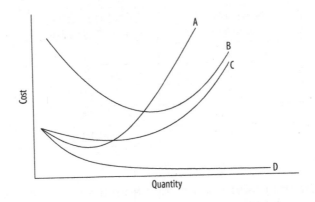

(A) Average total cost increases relative to average variable cost.

(B) Average fixed cost decreases as the quantity produced increases.

(C) Average variable cost decreases relative to average total cost.

(D) Marginal cost increases as the quantity produced increases.

(E) Average total cost decreases initially and then increases.

11. A firm is currently experiencing diseconomies of scale. What should the firm do to reduce its long-run average total cost?

(A) Increase output by increasing factory size.

(B) Increase output by decreasing factory size.

(C) Decrease output by increasing factory size.

(D) Decrease output by decreasing factory size.

(E) Increase output, but do not adjust the size of the factory.

12. A firm should do which of the following to maximize profits?

(A) Produce a quantity where total revenue equals total cost.

(B) Produce a quantity where marginal revenue is greater than marginal cost.

(C) Produce a quantity where total revenue is less than total cost.

(D) Produce a quantity where marginal revenue is less than marginal cost.

(E) Produce a quantity where marginal revenue equals marginal cost.

13. Assume a firm produces tomatoes in a perfectly competitive market. An increase in the market demand for tomatoes will have what effect on the tomato market's output and on the firm's output in the short run and then in the long run?

(A) Output in the market and at the firm will increase in the short run, and in the long run market output will increase further while the firm's output decreases.

(B) Output in the market and at the firm will increase in the short run and in the long run.

(C) Output in the market will increase while the firm's output decreases in the short run, but in the long run both the market and the firm will experience an increase in output.

(D) Output in the market will decrease in the short run while the firm's output will increase, but in the long run output in the market and the firm will increase.

(E) Output in the market and at the firm will decrease in the short run, but in the long run market output and the firm's output will both increase.

Question 14 refers to the
following graph.

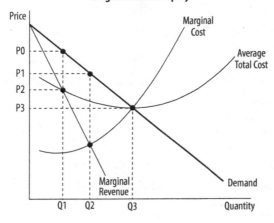

14. This firm will maximize profits at which quantity (Q) and price (P)?

(A) Q1, P0

(B) Q1, P1

(C) Q1, P2

(D) Q2, P1

(E) Q3, P3

15. Compared to a perfectly competitive market for electricity, a regulated natural monopoly which produces an allocatively efficient quantity of electricity does which of the following?

(A) Produces more output at a higher price

(B) Produces more output at a lower price

(C) Produces less output at a higher price

(D) Produces less output at a lower price

(E) Produces the same output at a higher price

16. A single-price monopolist discovers that it is now able to perfectly price discriminate. What will happen to each of the following as a result of the discovery?

Consumer Surplus	Profit	Deadweight Loss
(A) Increase	Increase	Increase
(B) Decrease	Increase	Increase
(C) Decrease	Decrease	Decrease
(D) Decrease	Decrease	Increase
(E) Decrease	Increase	Decrease

17. A monopolistically competitive firm will

(A) advertise to differentiate its products from the competition

(B) perfectly price discriminate because it has unlimited pricing power

(C) increase output when it faces more competition

(D) maximize profits by producing where marginal revenue exceeds marginal cost

(E) operate at a lower average total cost than a similarly sized firm in a perfectly competitive market

The payoff matrix shows the daily profit that could be earned by two profit-maximizing firms, Bob's and Chuck's, competing in an oligopolistic market.

	Chuck's (C) advertises	Chuck's (C) does not advertise
Bob's (B) advertises	(B) $100 (C) $150	(B) $110 (C) $100
Bob's (B) does not advertise	(B) $110 (C) $200	(B) $90 (C) $180

18. Identify which of the following statements is correct.

(A) Bob's dominant strategy is to advertise while Chuck's dominant strategy is not to advertise.

(B) Bob's and Chuck's both have a dominant strategy not to advertise.

(C) Bob's and Chuck's both have a dominant strategy to advertise.

(D) Bob's does not have a dominant strategy, but Chuck's has a dominant strategy not to advertise.

(E) Bob's does not have a dominant strategy, but Chuck's has a dominant strategy to advertise.

19. Determine which of the following combinations is a Nash equilibrium.

(A) Bob's advertises and Chuck's advertises.

(B) Bob's does not advertise and Chuck's advertises.

(C) Bob's advertises and Chuck's does not advertise.

(D) Bob's does not advertise and Chuck's does not advertise.

(E) There is no Nash equilibrium in the payoff matrix.

20. Assume a perfectly competitive market for good Y exists. Further assume that the market for labor is perfectly competitive. An increase in the price of good Y will result in which of the following changes in the market for labor?

Wage	Quantity of Labor Employed
(A) Increase	Decrease
(B) Increase	Increase
(C) Decrease	Increase
(D) Decrease	Decrease
(E) Increase	No Change

21. Which best explains why the marginal revenue product of labor equals the monetary value of the marginal product of labor for firms in a competitive output market?

(A) Marginal product is constant for firms in a perfectly competitive output market.

(B) Marginal product is increasing for firms in a perfectly competitive output market.

(C) Price is equal to marginal revenue for firms in a perfectly competitive output market.

(D) Price is equal to marginal product for firms in a perfectly competitive output market.

(E) Price is less than marginal revenue for firms in a perfectly competitive output market.

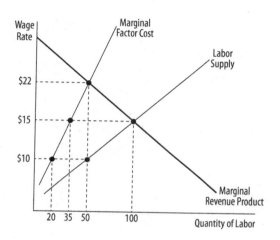

22. Compared to a firm facing a perfectly competitive labor
market, a firm with monopsony power in the labor
market will

(A) hire 50 fewer workers and pay a wage rate $7
higher

(B) hire 50 more workers and pay a wage rate $7
higher

(C) hire 65 fewer workers and pay the same wage rate

(D) hire 80 fewer workers and pay a wage rate $5 lower

(E) hire 50 fewer workers and pay a wage rate $5 lower

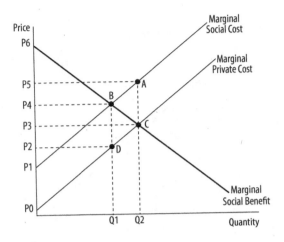

23. Assume that the market for a good creates a negative externality as shown in the graph. The presence of a negative externality creates which of the following?

(A) A market equilibrium price of P3, an equilibrium quantity of Q2, and deadweight loss equal to the area of triangle ABC.

(B) A market equilibrium price of P4, an equilibrium quantity of Q1, and deadweight loss equal to the area of triangle BCD.

(C) A market equilibrium price of P5, an equilibrium quantity of Q2, and total cost of P5 × Q2.

(D) A market equilibrium price of P2, an equilibrium quantity of Q1, and total revenue of P2 × Q1.

(E) A market equilibrium price of P3, an equilibrium quantity of Q2, and total cost of P3 × Q2.

24. Assume government officials want to mitigate the effect of the negative externality by incentivizing the socially optimal price and quantity in the market. The officials should do which of the following?

(A) Set a price ceiling at P3.

(B) Charge a per unit tax equal to P1 − P0 on producers.

(C) Charge a lump sum tax equal to P2 × Q1.

(D) Set a price floor at P2.

(E) Set a quota at Q2.

25. One source of income inequality in an economy is the level of tax progressivity. Which of the following shows taxes in order of progressivity from most regressive to most progressive?

(A) Flat rate tax of 10% on all household income, sales tax of 8% on all items sold to consumers, marginal income tax of 25% on household incomes above $65,000

(B) Flat rate tax of 10% on all household income, marginal income tax of 25% on household incomes above $65,000, sales tax of 8% on all items sold to consumers

(C) Marginal income tax of 25% on household incomes above $65,000, flat tax of 10% on all household income, sales tax of 8% on all items sold to consumers

(D) Sales tax of 8% on all items sold to consumers, marginal income tax of 25% on household incomes above $65,000, flat tax of 10% on all household income

(E) Sales tax of 8% on all items sold to consumers, flat tax of 10% on all household income, marginal income tax of 25% on household incomes above $65,000

ANSWERS AND EXPLANATIONS

1. (E)

Carlo's opportunity cost of planting trees is 1 tree per 6 shrubs, and his opportunity cost of planting shrubs is 1 shrub per ⅙ of a tree. Bella's opportunity cost of planting trees is 1 tree per 5 shrubs, and her opportunity cost of planting shrubs is 1 shrub per ⅕ of a tree. Carlo has a lower opportunity cost of planting shrubs because 1 shrub per ⅙ of a tree is lower than Bella's 1 shrub per ⅕ of a tree, so Carlo has a comparative advantage in planting shrubs. Bella has a lower opportunity cost of planting trees because 1 tree per 5 shrubs is lower than Carlo's 1 tree per 6 shrubs, so Bella has a comparative advantage in planting trees.

(A) and (D) are incorrect because market economies and free enterprise economies rely on decentralized markets to allocate goods and services rather than a central planner. (B) is incorrect because mixed economies rely on a combination of central planning and markets to answer the questions of what to produce, how to produce, and for whom to produce. (C) is incorrect because traditional economies rely on societal tradition and cultural practices to determine what is produced, how it is produced, and for whom it is produced. (E) is correct because a command economy relies solely on government to determine what is produced, how it is produced, and for whom it is produced.

2. (C)

(A) is incorrect because point B is on the production possibilities curve. (B) is incorrect because point B is on the production possibilities curve, and point E reflects an increase in consumer goods rather than capital goods. Choice (C) is correct because point F is inside the production possibilities curve to reflect the assumption that the economy is not fully employing all of its available resources, and the move to point B reflects an increase in the production of capital goods. (D) is incorrect because point D is on the production possibilities curve. (E) is incorrect because F to C illustrates an increase in the production of consumer goods rather than capital goods.

3. (D)

Choice (A) is incorrect because Carlo only has a comparative advantage in planting shrubs. (B) is incorrect because Carlo's only comparative advantage is in planting shrubs. (C) is incorrect because Bella's comparative advantage is in planting trees. (D) is correct because Carlo plants shrubs at a lower opportunity cost than Bella, and Bella plants trees at a lower opportunity cost than Carlo. (E) is incorrect because Carlo's only comparative advantage is in planting shrubs.

4. (D)

Demand for good X is relatively elastic because the percentage change in the quantity demanded is greater than the percentage increase in the price of good X. Good Y is a substitute for good X because an increase in the price of good X, results in an increase in the quantity demanded for good Y.

(A) is incorrect because the price elasticity of demand for good X is relatively elastic and the cross-price elasticity of demand for good X relative to good Y indicates the goods are substitutes rather than complements. (B) is incorrect because the price elasticity of demand for good X is relatively elastic. (C) is incorrect because the cross-price elasticity of demand for good X relative to good Y indicates the goods are substitutes rather than complements. (D) is correct because the price elasticity of demand for good X is relatively elastic, and the cross-price elasticity of demand for good X relative to good Y indicates the goods are substitutes. (E) is incorrect because the price elasticity of demand for good X is relatively elastic and there is insufficient evidence to indicate that good Y is a perfect substitute for good X.

5. (D)

A good is inferior if its income elasticity of demand is negative. Increased consumer incomes result in less demand for inferior goods.

(A) is incorrect because consumer income does not affect supply, but it does affect demand. (B) is incorrect because consumer income does not affect supply, but it does affect demand. (C) is incorrect because an increase in consumer income would only result in an increase for normal goods and not inferior goods. (D) is correct because an increase in consumer income results in a decrease in demand for inferior goods. (E) is incorrect because consumer income does not affect supply, and an increase in income would not result in an increased demand for inferior goods.

6. **(B)**

Choice (A) is incorrect because increasing the price producers charge for good X will result in the quantity supplied still being greater than the quantity demanded. (B) is correct because when the quantity supplied exceeds the quantity demanded, producers compete with each other by lowering their price to encourage consumers to buy more of the good and eliminate the temporary surplus. (C) is incorrect because an effective price floor would prevent the market from responding to the surplus condition. (D) is incorrect because an effective price ceiling would not affect a market currently experiencing a price above the market equilibrium price. (E) is incorrect because the substitution effect would result in less demand for good X.

7. **(C)**

Choice (A) is incorrect because increased per unit labor productivity increases supply and does not affect demand. (B) is incorrect because increased per unit labor productivity increases supply and does not affect demand. (C) is correct because increased per unit labor productivity reduces the per unit cost of production which increases the supply, but the presence of an effective price floor prevents the price from decreasing. (D) is incorrect because increased per unit labor productivity has the opposite effect on supply. (E) is incorrect because increased per unit labor productivity increases supply and does not affect demand.

8. (C)

Choice (A) is incorrect because removing the tariff reduces the deadweight loss and increases the quantity imported. (B) is incorrect because removing the tariff increases the quantity imported. (C) is correct because removing the tariff reduces the price from Pw + Tariff to Pw. The result is increased consumer surplus, decreased producer surplus, elimination of deadweight loss, and an increase in the quantity of imports. (D) is incorrect because removing the tariff increases consumer surplus, decreases producer surplus, and eliminates the deadweight loss. (E) is incorrect because removing the tariff increases consumer surplus and decreases producer surplus.

9. (D)

A production function is divided into three distinct stages based on the change in total product and the change in marginal product. Stage 1 is characterized by increasing marginal returns as total product and marginal product both increase. Stage 2 is characterized by diminishing marginal returns as total product increases while marginal product decreases. Stage 3 is characterized by negative marginal returns as both total product and marginal product decrease.

(A) is incorrect because the addition of the first worker results in increasing marginal returns as total product and marginal product increases from 0 to 3. (B) is incorrect because the addition of the second worker results in increasing returns as total product increases to 7 and marginal product increases to 4. (C) is incorrect because the addition of the third worker results in increasing marginal returns as total product increases to 12 and marginal product increases to 5. (D) is correct because the addition of the fourth worker results in diminishing marginal returns as total product increases to 15 but marginal product decreases to 3. (E) is incorrect because marginal returns had already decreased with the addition of the fourth worker.

10. (B)

In the graph for this question, curve A represents marginal cost, curve B represents average total cost, curve C represents average variable cost, and curve D represents average fixed cost. Marginal cost is the change in total cost divided by the change in output. Average total cost is the sum of average variable cost and average fixed cost. Average variable cost is total variable cost divided by output. Average fixed cost is total fixed cost divided by output.

(A) is incorrect because as the quantity produced increases, average total cost and average variable cost initially decrease and then both increase, with average variable cost increasing at a faster rate than average total cost. (B) is correct because as the quantity produced increases, average fixed cost approaches zero. Average variable cost and average total cost begin to converge because average total cost is the sum of average variable cost and the quickly diminishing average fixed cost. (C) is incorrect because average variable cost increases relative to average total cost throughout its entire range. (D) is incorrect because although marginal cost is indeed increasing, it is not the cause of the convergence between average total cost and average variable cost. (E) is incorrect because although average total cost initially decreases then increases, this does not explain why it converges with average variable cost.

11. (D)

A firm experiences diseconomies of scale when the size of its physical capital is so large that it results in increasing long-run average total cost. (A) is incorrect because increasing factory size will result in increased long-run average total cost for a firm already experiencing diseconomies of scale. (B) is incorrect because increasing output does not result in lower long-run average total cost for a firm already experiencing diseconomies of scale. (C) is incorrect because increasing factory size will result in increased long-run average total cost for a firm already experiencing diseconomies of scale. (D) is correct because decreasing output and factory size results in the firm experiencing lower long-run average total cost.

(E) is incorrect because increasing output results in higher long-run average total cost for a firm already experiencing diseconomies of scale.

12. (E)

Choice (A) is incorrect because total revenue equal to total cost results in zero profit. (B) is incorrect because when marginal revenue is greater than marginal cost there are still profitable transactions that could take place. (C) is incorrect because when total revenue is less than total cost, the firm is experiencing a loss. (D) is incorrect because firms are incurring losses on the additional output produced beyond the level at which marginal revenue equaled marginal cost. (E) is correct because when marginal revenue equals marginal cost, the total revenue is at its maximum positive distance from total cost.

13. (A)

Choice (A) is correct because increased demand in the market for tomatoes results in both a greater equilibrium price and quantity for the market in the short run. In response to the higher market price, the firm will increase its output of tomatoes as the higher market price results in higher marginal revenue for the firm. Since the firm maximizes profits by producing at the point where marginal revenue equals marginal cost, the increased marginal revenue encourages the firm to produce more to maximize profits. The result is that firms in the tomato market earn economic profits. In the long run, the presence of economic profits in the industry attracts the entrance of new firms to the market. These new firms increase the supply of tomatoes in the market, which increases the equilibrium quantity but reduces the equilibrium price. Firms already in the market now face more competition, falling prices, and a smaller share of total sales, leading them to reduce their output to avoid losses. (B) is incorrect because in the long run, the entrance of new firms eliminates economic profits and results in lower output for each individual firm. (C) is incorrect because in the short run, capital is fixed and new firms are unable to enter the market to meet the demand, so existing firms increase their output in response to the higher market price and higher marginal revenue. The rest of the answer is a non sequitur. (D) is incorrect because an increase in demand for a normal good results in a higher equilibrium quantity in the market. The rest of the answer is a non sequitur. (E) is incorrect because an increase in demand for a normal good results in a higher equilibrium price and quantity in the market, and in the short run results in a higher output for a profit maximizing firm. The rest of the answer is a non sequitur.

14. (D)

Firms maximize profits when they follow the profit-maximizing rule of producing where marginal revenue equals marginal cost.

(A), (B), and (C) are incorrect because Q1 is associated with marginal revenue being greater than marginal cost. (D) is correct because Q2 is associated with marginal revenue being equal to marginal cost. The demand price at that quantity is P1. (E) is incorrect because Q3 is associated with marginal revenue being less than marginal cost.

15. (B)

Regulated natural monopoly is encouraged by government when the result is lower average total cost for the same amount of output that would otherwise be produced in a competitive market. This happens because natural monopolies experience significant economies of scale.

(A) is incorrect because a regulated natural monopoly that is allocatively efficient will produce at a lower price because of its economy of scale. (B) is correct because a regulated natural monopoly which produces an allocatively efficient quantity, is producing more output at a lower price than any one firm in a competitive market would be able to do. (C) is incorrect because the regulated natural monopoly will produce more output at a lower price than any one firm in a competitive market would be able to do. (D) is incorrect because the regulated natural monopoly will produce more output than a smaller firm in a competitive market. (E) is incorrect because the regulated natural monopoly will produce more output at a lower price than a smaller firm in a competitive market.

16. (E)

Choice (A) is incorrect because perfect price discrimination eliminates consumer surplus and deadweight loss. (B) is incorrect because perfect price discrimination eliminates deadweight loss. (C) is incorrect because perfect price discrimination increases profits for the firm. (D) is incorrect because perfect price discrimination increases profits and eliminates deadweight loss for the firm/market. (E) is correct because a monopoly able to perfectly price discriminate, eliminates consumer surplus and deadweight loss for the market and increases profits for the firm.

17. (A)

Choice (A) is correct because monopolistically competitive firms advertise to differentiate their products from other competitors in order to charge a higher price for their product or service. (B) is incorrect because monopolistically competitive firms still face competition and are unable to perfectly price discriminate. Also, consumer demand limits pricing power for the firm as well. (C) is incorrect because increased competition reduces the demand for the monopolistically competitive firm's output, resulting in less output. (D) is incorrect because firms maximize profits by producing where marginal revenue *equals* marginal cost. (E) is incorrect because monopolistically competitive firms do not operate at the minimum of average total cost like perfectly competitive firms.

18. (E)

Choice (A) is incorrect because Bob's does not have a dominant strategy. Bob's profit-maximizing decision is dependent upon Chuck's strategy. Chuck's dominant strategy is to advertise because independent of Bob's decision, Chuck's maximizes profits by advertising. (B) is incorrect because Bob's does not have a dominant strategy. Bob's profit-maximizing decision is dependent upon Chuck's strategy. Chuck's dominant strategy is to advertise because independent of Bob's decision, Chuck's maximizes profits by advertising. (C) is incorrect because Bob's does not have a dominant strategy. Bob's profit-maximizing decision is dependent upon Chuck's strategy. (D) is incorrect because Chuck's dominant strategy is to advertise to maximize profits. (E) is correct because Bob's profit-maximizing strategy is dependent upon Chuck's strategy. Chuck's maximizes profits by advertising independent of Bob's decision.

19. (B)

Choice (A) is incorrect because Bob's is better off not advertising if Chuck's advertises. (B) is correct because neither firm has an incentive to change their decision given the other firm's decision. (C) is incorrect because Chuck's is better off advertising given Bob's decision to advertise. (D) is incorrect because Bob's is better off advertising given Chuck's decision not to advertise, and Chuck's is better off advertising given Bob's decision not to advertise. (E) is incorrect because there is one outcome at which neither firm has an incentive to change their decision, so there is a Nash equilibrium in the payoff matrix.

20. (B)

Choice (A) is incorrect because an increase in the price of good Y will increase the marginal revenue product of labor for producers of Y, given a competitive labor market which results in an increased quantity of labor employed. (B) is correct because an increase in the price of good Y will increase the marginal revenue product of labor for producers of Y, given a competitive labor market which results in an increased wage rate and an increased quantity of labor employed. (C) is incorrect because an increase in the price of good Y will increase the marginal revenue product of labor for producers of good Y, resulting in an increased wage rate. (D) is incorrect because an increase in the price of good Y will increase the marginal revenue product of labor for producers of Y, given a competitive labor market which results in an increased wage rate and an increased quantity of labor employed. (E) is incorrect because an increase in the price of good Y will increase the marginal revenue product of labor for producers of Y, given a competitive labor market which results not only in an increase in the wage rate, but also an increase in the quantity of labor employed.

21. (C)

Choice (A) is incorrect because marginal product varies according to the firm's production function. (B) is incorrect because marginal product eventually diminishes and decreases as the firm continues to employ more labor. Choice (C) is correct because in a competitive output market, the market equilibrium price becomes the individual firm's marginal revenue given that marginal revenue product equals the marginal product × marginal revenue. (D) is incorrect because marginal product is not measured with money. (E) is incorrect because price equals marginal revenue for all firms in a perfectly competitive market.

22. (E)

In order to maximize their profits in factor markets, firms will hire workers up to the point the where the marginal revenue product of labor is equal to the marginal factor cost.

(A) is incorrect because the wage rate is based on the supply price of $10 rather than the marginal revenue product of labor price of $22. (B) is incorrect because fewer workers are hired in monopsony rather than more, and the wage rate is lower, not higher. (C) is incorrect because the quantity of 35 is not associated with marginal revenue product equal to marginal factor cost. (D) is incorrect because the quantity of 20 is not associated with marginal revenue product equal to marginal factor cost. (E) is correct because the firm employs 50 units of labor associated with marginal revenue product equal to marginal factor cost, whereas given a competitive labor market, in which the marginal factor cost equals the supply of labor, firms would employ 100 units of labor. Furthermore, the supply price of labor at 50 units is $10, which is $5 less than the competitive equilibrium wage of $15.

23. (A)

Choice (A) is correct because market equilibrium price and quantity occur where marginal private cost equals marginal benefit, and the deadweight loss equal to the triangle ABS is created because the socially optimal price and quantity occur where marginal social cost equals marginal benefit. Resources are overallocated towards the good at Q2, creating a deadweight loss. (B) is incorrect because P4 and Q1 are socially optimal and do not result in deadweight loss. (C) is incorrect because P5 is the marginal social cost at the market equilibrium, but the price associated with market equilibrium is P3. (D) is incorrect because P2 is not associated with marginal private cost equal to marginal social benefit and the resultant deadweight loss. (E) is incorrect because the total explicit and implicit costs in the market are in fact, P3 × Q2 creating a total cost to society of P3 × Q2.

24. (B)

Choice (A) is incorrect because a price ceiling at P3 is non-binding and will have no impact on market equilibrium. (B) is correct because charging a per unit tax equal to P1 − P0 forces producers to internalize the negative externality and results in a socially optimal outcome where the marginal social cost equals the marginal social benefit. (C) is incorrect because a lump sum tax will not affect the marginal cost. (D) is incorrect because a price floor of P2 would be ineffective because it is below both the market equilibrium price and the socially optimal price. (E) is incorrect because a quota at Q2 would not reduce the quantity to the socially optimal quantity of Q1.

25. (E)

Tax progressivity is measured by determining what fraction of household income is taxed. If the fraction paid for households with low incomes is relatively higher than the fraction paid by households with high incomes, then the tax is regressive. If the tax takes the same fraction from all households regardless of income, then the tax is proportional. If the fraction paid in taxes is higher for households with relatively higher income, then the tax is progressive.

Sales taxes are regressive because they place a larger burden on low- versus high-income households. For example, assume an 8% sales tax on a pair of $100 shoes: The resulting $8 in taxes represents a larger relative burden for households with low incomes than it does for households with high incomes. Flat taxes are proportional because they take the same fraction of income from households regardless of the level of household income. For example, assume a 10% flat tax on household income: Regardless of income each household will only pay 10% of their income in taxes.

Marginal income taxes are progressive because as household income increases, the fraction of household income paid in taxes increases. For example, assume a government charges households two different marginal tax rates based on household income. Further assume the first marginal rate is 10% of household income between $0 and $65,000 and the second marginal rate is 25% of household income between $65,001 and up. A household earning $20,000 will pay a 10% marginal rate and 10% average rate of $2,000 in taxes. A household earning $100,000 will pay 10% on the first $65,000, or $6,500 plus 25% on the difference [25% × ($100,000 − $65,000)] or $8,750, which totals $15,250, creating an average tax burden of 15.25%.

(A) is incorrect because a sales tax of 8% on all items sold to consumers is more regressive than a flat-rate tax of 10% on all household income. (B) is incorrect because the sales tax of 8% on all items sold to consumers is more regressive than either the marginal income tax of 25% on household incomes above $65,000 and the flat-rate tax of 10% on all household income. (C) is incorrect because the flat-rate tax and the sales tax are more regressive than the marginal income tax. (D) is incorrect because the flat tax on all household income is more regressive than the marginal income tax of 25% on household incomes above $65,000. (E) is correct because sales taxes are regressive, flat taxes are proportional, and the marginal income tax is progressive.

Mastering the Free-Response Questions

The AP® Microeconomics exam's free-response section is made up of three questions. You have ten minutes to read and plan your answers. Then you will have 50 minutes to answer all three questions.

I. Think Like an Economist

A. Don't waste time. The first question is worth half the credit for the free-response section and should be given about half of the allotted 50 minutes. The remaining time should be spent on answering the two shorter questions that are each worth one quarter of the free-response points.

B. *Never* skip a question.

1. It's expected that you answer all three free-response questions. Answer all the parts of the questions and structure your response to mirror the structure of the question.

2. Skipping an entire question will not get you any points. Even if your answer is incomplete, you can still earn points. You don't lose points for trying all the parts.

3. If a graph helps answer the question, draw it and be sure to label it correctly. Often if there is a shift or change in a graph, you can earn half or more of the points for setting up the graph correctly even if you get the shift backwards.

C. When a question asks you about what happened to price and quantity, *graph it!* Graphing is required on many free-response questions. If you are asked for a correctly labeled graph, you will sacrifice credit if you don't provide the graph for which the exam graders are looking.

D. Once you've completed the free-response section, go back over the questions. Use the following reflection questions to help you write a concise and correct answer:

    1. Does my response answer the question that was asked?

    2. Did I identify the question I was answering?

    3. If I was asked to *show* using a graph, did I label the graph correctly?

    4. Did I contradict myself in any part of the answer?

    5. If the question (or part of a question) stated *explain*, did I always provide a reason?

The AP® Microeconomics exam is unlike other social studies exams for many reasons. One major difference between AP® Micro and the AP® history exams is the amount of writing necessary to answer the free-response question. AP® Micro emphasizes analysis, logic, and graphing over prose or the ability to write a thesis. Keep your answers short, simple, and to-the-point. Avoid writing more than one sentence when answering a question. If you're unsure of how to answer a question, don't write every fact you know about economics. Take some time to think about the most direct answer and practice how you'll explain it. Pick a direction and stick with it. Consistency is very important on the AP® Micro exam.

II. Free-Response Strategies

A. Write neatly. Remember, your free-response answers will be graded by people who have to read handwritten student answers for eight hours a day. A saying among the economics experts at the AP® Reading is: "Easy to read, easy to grade."

B. As you look over the questions during the ten-minute planning period, underline the verbs in the questions. These verbs are the keys to understanding what's expected from you in an answer. The following verbs will most likely show up on the free-response section of the exam: *calculate, define, draw, explain, identify, indicate, label,* and *show.*

1. *Calculate* means to add, subtract, multiply, or divide numbers and/or correctly apply a formula to solve a problem. **Always show your work.**

   i. A good sign that you are doing a problem correctly is that you don't feel the need for a calculator.

   ii. The answer to a problem is usually a nice whole number or an easy fraction. If you start getting irrational numbers or feel the need for a graphing calculator, then you're probably doing the problem the wrong way.

2. *Draw a correctly labeled graph* means to reproduce a graph from memory.

   i. Be sure to make your graphs large and easily readable. A graph should occupy one-half of the page and should be clearly labeled. When in doubt, over-label the graph.

   ii. Clearly show changes in graphs by using arrows and subscripts. Be careful to maintain consistency. For example, an increase in demand leads to an increase in price and quantity, so there should be no arrows pointing down or to the left when illustrating this specific change. If you are consistent about labeling and D1 shifts to D2, making the quantity increase from Q1 to Q2 and price from P1 to P2, your graph will be more likely to earn all the credit you deserve.

3. *Explain* usually follows after "what will happen . . ." or "indicate." In the context of the exam, *explain* means to show why a cause-and-effect relationship exists between two variables. The graders are looking to see if they can award you credit for the reason involved. (A good way to check your answer is to see if you've used "because.")

An example of an "explain" question:

> Assume that cheese is a normal good. Indicate the effect of an increase in consumers' income on the price and quantity of cheese. Explain?

The answer would be:

> The price and quantity of cheese increase because an increase in consumer income results in an increase in demand for normal goods.

4. *Identify* means to provide a single word or concept that answers the question.

5. *Indicate* means to provide a direction for some change that the question is asking about. *Indicate* questions usually have two possible answers: *increase* or *decrease*.

6. *Label* is directing you to write a word, letter, or arrow on a graph that you have already drawn which shows that you understand the change that has occurred in the graph.

7. *Show, label, plot, or indicate* means to make a change to a graph by adding new information such as a new curve and then to demonstrate the effects of the change on the horizontal and vertical axes. Typically, you will be told which graph to show your effect. Use arrows to clarify what was there before and what is new. Even though it isn't usually required, you are welcome to write a one-sentence explanation next to or beneath the graph telling what happened if you feel it isn't clear.

Economics Glossary

Aggregate demand—shows the total quantity of goods and services consumed at different price and output levels.

Aggregate demand/aggregate supply (AD/AS) model—uses aggregate demand and aggregate supply to determine and explain price level, real domestic output, disposable income, and employment.

Aggregate expenditure—all spending for final goods and services in an economy: $C + I_g + G + Xn = AE$.

Allocative efficiency—distribution of resources among firms and industries to obtain production quantities of the products most wanted by society (consumers); where marginal cost equals marginal benefit.

Appreciation (of the dollar)—an increase in the value of the dollar relative to the currency of another nation, so that a dollar buys more of the foreign currency and thus foreign goods become cheaper; critical to long-run trade equilibrium.

Asset—items of monetary value owned by a firm or individual; opposite is *liability*.

Average fixed cost (AFC)—firm's total fixed cost divided by output.

Average product—total output produced per unit of a resource employed (total product divided by the quantity of input).

Average total cost (ATC)—firm's total cost divided by output, equal to average fixed cost plus average variable cost (AFC + AVC = ATC).

Average variable cost (AVC)—firm's total variable cost divided by output.

Balance of payments account—summary of a nation's current account and its financial account.

Balance of trade—a nation's current account balance; net exports.

Balance sheet—statement of the assets and liabilities that determines a firm's net (solvency).

Barrier to entry—artificial prevention of the entry of firms into an industry.

Bond—financial instrument through which a borrower (corporate or government) is contracted to pay the principal at a specified interest rate at a specific date (maturity) in the future; promissory note.

Breakeven point—output at which a (competitive) firm's total cost and total revenue are equal (TR = TC); an output at which a firm has neither an economic profit nor a loss, at which it earns only a normal profit.

Budget deficit—amount by which the spending of the (federal) government exceeds its tax revenues in any year.

Budget surplus—amount by which the tax revenues of the (federal) government exceed its spending in any year.

Capital—resources (buildings, machinery, and equipment) used to produce goods and services; also called *investment goods*.

Capital account—section of a nation's international balance-of-payments balance sheet that records foreign purchases of U.S. assets (money in) and U.S. purchases of foreign assets (money out).

Capital account inflow (outflow)—reflects the net difference between foreign funds invested in the home country minus the domestic funds invested in the foreign country; component of the balance of payments account.

Capitalism—free market economic system in which property is privately owned and the invisible forces of supply and demand set price and quantity.

Cartel—overt agreement among firms (or countries) in an industry to fix the price of a product and establish output quotas.

Change in demand—change in the quantity demanded of a good or service at all prices; a shift of the demand curve to the left (decrease) or right (increase).

Change in supply—change in the quantity supplied of a good or service at all prices; a shift of the supply curve to the left (decrease) or right (increase).

Circular flow model—flow of resource inputs from households to businesses and of goods and services (g/s) from businesses to households. A flow in the opposite direction of money—businesses to households for inputs and from households to businesses for g/s—occurs simultaneously.

Comparative advantage—determines specialization and exchange rate for trade between nations; based on the nation with the lower relative or comparative cost of production.

Competition—Adam Smith's requirement for success of a free market, a market of independent buyers and sellers competing with one another; includes ease of access to and exit from the marketplace.

Complementary goods—goods that are used together, so if the price of one falls, the demand for the other decreases as well (and vice versa).

Consumer price index (CPI)—index that measures the prices of a set "basket" of some 300 goods and services bought by a "typical" consumer; used by government as a main indicator of the rate of inflation.

Consumer surplus—that portion of the demand curve that lies above the equilibrium price level and denotes those consumers that would be willing to buy the goods and services at higher price levels.

Contractionary fiscal policy—combination of government reduction in spending and a net increase in taxes, for the purpose of decreasing aggregate demand, lowering price levels, and thus controlling inflation.

Corporation—legal entity ("like a person") chartered by a state or the federal government; limits liability for business debt to the assets of the firm.

Cost-push inflation—when an increase in resource costs shifts the aggregate supply curve inward, resulting in an increase in the price level and unemployment; also termed *stagflation*.

Cross elasticity of demand—ratio of the percentage change in quantity demanded of one good to the percentage change in the price of another good. If the coefficient is positive, the two goods are substitute. If the coefficient is negative, they are considered complementary.

Crowding-out effect—caused by the federal government's increased borrowing in the money market that results in a rise in interest rates. The rise in interest rates results in a decrease in gross business domestic investment (I_g), which reduces the effectiveness of expansionary fiscal policy.

Current account—section in a nation's international balance of payments that records its exports and imports of goods and services, its net investment income, and its net transfers; component of the balance of payments account.

Cyclical deficit—government budget deficit caused by a recession and the resultant decline in tax revenues.

Cyclical unemployment—type of unemployment caused by recession; less than full employment aggregate demand.

Deadweight loss (efficiency loss)—the foregone total societal surplus associated with the levy of a tax that discourages what had heretofore been a mutually advantageous market transaction.

Deflation—decline in the economy's price level; indicates contraction in business cycle or may signal expansion of total output (aggregate supply moves to the right).

Demand—the quantity of a good or service that buyers wish to buy at various prices.

Depreciation (of the dollar)—decrease in the value of the dollar relative to another currency, so that the dollar buys a smaller amount of the foreign currency and therefore the price of foreign goods increases; tends to reduce imports and increase exports.

Determinants of demand—factors other than price that alter (shift) the quantities demanded of a good or service.

Determinants of supply—factors other than price that alter (shift) the quantities supplied of a good or service.

Discount rate—interest rate that the Federal Reserve Banks charge on the loans they make to banks (different from the federal funds rate).

Disposable income—personal income minus personal taxes; income available for consumption expenditures and saving.

Durable good—consumer good with an expected life (use) of three or more years; decrease in sales indicates recession, as contraction affects these goods before nondurables.

Economic efficiency—use of the minimum necessary inputs to obtain the most societally beneficial quantity of goods and services; employs both productive and allocative efficiency.

Economic profit—total revenue of a firm minus its economic costs (both explicit and implicit costs); also termed *pure profit* and *above-normal profit*.

Economies of scale—savings in the average total cost of production as the firm expands the size of plant (its output) in the long run.

Elastic demand—product or resource demand whose price elasticity is greater than 1. This means that the resulting percentage change in quantity demanded is greater than the percentage change in price.

Elastic supply—product or resource supply whose price elasticity is greater than 1. This means that the resulting percentage change in quantity supplied is greater than the percentage change in price.

Equilibrium price—price at which the quantity demanded and the quantity supplied are equal (intersect), shelves clear, and price stability occurs.

Equilibrium quantity—quantity demanded and supplied at the equilibrium price.

Excess capacity—plant resources underused when imperfectly competitive firms produce less output than that associated with achieving minimum average total cost.

Expansionary fiscal policy—combination of government increases in spending and a net decrease in taxes, for the purpose of increasing aggregate demand, increasing output and disposable income, and lowering unemployment.

Expected rate of return—profit a firm anticipates it will obtain by purchasing capital goods; influences investment demand for money.

Factors of production—resources: land, capital, and entrepreneurial ability.

Federal funds rate—the interest rate banks and other depository institutions charge one another on overnight loans made out of their excess reserves; targeted by monetary policy.

Financial account (capital account)—the difference between a country's sale of assets to foreigners and its purchase of foreign assets; component of the balance of payments account.

Fixed cost—any cost that remains constant when the firm changes its output.

Fixed exchange rate—rate of currency exchange that is set, prevented from rising or falling with changes in currency supply and demand; opposite of floating exchange rate.

Frictional unemployment—unemployment caused by workers' voluntarily changing jobs or workers' being between jobs.

Full employment unemployment rate—natural rate of unemployment when there is no cyclical unemployment. In the United States, it equals between 4 percent and 5 percent, because some frictional and structural unemployment is unavoidable.

Gross domestic product (GDP)—total market value of all final goods and services produced annually within the boundaries of the United States, whether by U.S. or foreign-supplied resources.

Horizontal merger—merger into a single firm of two firms that produce the same product and sell it in the same geographic market.

Hyperinflation—a very rapid rise in the price level; an extremely high rate of inflation.

Imperfect competition—all market structures except pure competition; includes monopoly, monopolistic competition, and oligopoly.

Implicit cost—the monetary income a firm sacrifices when it uses a resource it owns rather than supplying the resource in the market; equal to what the resource could have earned in the best-paying alternative employment; includes a normal profit.

Indifference curve—curve showing the different combinations of two products that yield the same satisfaction or utility to a consumer.

Inelastic demand—product or resource demand for which the elasticity coefficient for price is less than 1. This means the resulting percentage change in quantity demanded is less than the percentage change in price.

Inelastic supply—product or resource supply for which the price elasticity coefficient is less than 1. The percentage change in quantity supplied is less than the percentage change in price.

Inferior good—a good or service the consumption of which declines as income rises (and vice versa), with price remaining constant.

Inflation—rise in the general level of prices.

Inflation (rational) expectation—a key determinant that impacts the loanable funds market for both borrowers and lenders.

Inflationary gap—amount by which the aggregate expenditure and schedule must shift downward to decrease the nominal gross domestic product (GDP) to its full employment noninflationary level.

Interest—payment for the use of borrowed money.

Inventories—goods that have been produced but remain unsold.

Inverse relationship—the relationship between two variables that change in opposite directions; for example, product price and quantity demanded.

Kinked demand curve—demand curve for a noncollusive oligopolist, which is based on the assumption that rivals will follow a price decrease and ignore a price increase.

Law of demand—the principle that, other things being equal, an increase in the price of a product will reduce the quantity of that product demanded, and conversely for a decrease in price.

Law of diminishing marginal utility—the principle that as a consumer increases the consumption of a good or service (g/s), the marginal utility obtained from each additional unit of the g/s decreases.

Law of diminishing returns—the principle that as successive increments of a variable resource are added to a fixed resource, the marginal product of the variable resource will eventually decrease.

Law of increasing opportunity costs—the principle that as the production of a good increases, the opportunity cost of producing an additional unit rises.

Law of supply—the principle that, other things being equal, an increase in the price of a product will increase the quantity of that product supplied, and conversely for a price decrease.

Liability—a debt with a monetary value; an amount owed by a firm or an individual.

Liquidity—the ease with which an asset can be converted—quickly—into cash with little or no loss of purchasing power. Money is said to be perfectly liquid, whereas other assets have a lesser degree of liquidity.

Loanable funds market—a conceptual market wherein the demand for money is determined by borrowers and the supply is determined by lenders. Market equilibrium prices the interest rate.

Long run—time frame necessary for producers to alter resource inputs and increase or decrease output; time frame necessary for adjustments to be made as a result of shifts in aggregate demand and supply.

Lorenz curve—a model that demonstrates the cumulative percentage of population and their cumulative share of income; used to show shifts in income distribution across population over time.

M_1, M_2, M_3—money supply measurements that increasingly broaden the definition of money measured; critical to monetarism and interest rates.

Macroeconomics—the portion of economics concerned with the overall performance of the economy; focused on aggregate demand–aggregate supply relationship, and the resultant output, income, employment, and price levels.

Marginal benefit—change in total benefit that results from the consumption of one more unit of output.

Marginal cost—change in total cost that results from the sale of one more unit of output.

Marginal product—change in total output relative to the change in resource input.

Marginal propensity to consume—change in consumption spending relative to a change in income.

Marginal propensity to save—change in saving relative to a change in income.

Marginal revenue—change in total revenue that results from the sale of one more unit of product.

Marginal revenue cost (MRC)—change in total cost with the addition of one more unit of resource input for production.

Marginal revenue product (MRP)—change in total revenue with the addition of one more unit of resource input for production.

Marginal utility—the use a consumer gains from the addition of one more unit of a good or service.

Market failure—the inability of the free market to provide public goods; over- or underallocation of goods or services that have negative/positive externalities; used to justify government intervention.

Microeconomics—portion of economics concerned with the individual elements that make up the economy: households, firms, government, and resource input prices.

Monetary policy—policy basis on which the Federal Reserve influences interest rates through manipulation of the money supply to promote price stability, full employment, and productivity growth.

Money—any article (paper note, metal coin) generally accepted as having value in exchange for a good or service.

Money supply—defined, measured, and reported as M_1, M_2, M_3.

Monopsony—a market structure in which there is only one buyer of a resource input or good or service.

MR = MC principle—law stating that to maximize profit and minimize loss, a firm will produce at the output level where the marginal revenue is equal to the marginal cost.

MRP = MRC formula—equation showing that to maximize profit and minimize loss, a firm will employ a resource input quantity when the marginal revenue product is equal to the marginal resource cost of the resource input.

Multiplier—the effect that a change in one of the four components of aggregate expenditure has on gross domestic product (GDP).

Nash equilibrium—a condition in a payoff matrix where neither player has an incentive to change their strategy.

Natural monopoly—an industry in which the economy of scale is so large that one producer is the most efficient least-cost producer; usually regulated by government.

Natural rate of unemployment—frictional and structural unemployment, the full employment rate, zero cyclical unemployment.

Net export effect—any monetary or fiscal policy action is magnified (+ or −) by the effect that the change in U.S. dollar value (interest rates affect exchange rates) has on import and export prices.

Nominal—any economic measurement that is not adjusted for inflation.

Nominal interest rate—the interest rate that is not adjusted for inflation.

Normal good—a good or service (g/s) the consumption of which increases as income increases (opposite of inferior g/s).

Normal profit—where price equals average total cost, and cost includes the implicit cost of entrepreneurial value.

Oligopoly—a market structure in which a few firms have a large market share and sell differentiated products. In oligopolies, firms tend to have large economies of scale, pricing is mutually dependent, and price wars can occur; there is a kinked demand curve.

Perfectly elastic demand—infinite quantity demanded at a particular price; graphed as a straight horizontal line.

Perfectly elastic supply—infinite quantity supplied at a particular price; graphed as a straight horizontal line.

Perfectly inelastic demand—quantity demanded does not change in response to a change in price; graphed as a vertical straight line.

Perfectly inelastic supply—quantity supplied does not change in response to a change in price; graphed as a horizontal straight line.

Phillips curve (short run)—a model that demonstrates the inverse relationship between unemployment (horizontal) and inflation (vertical axis).

Phillips curve (long run)—a model demonstrating that, after inflation expectations have been adjusted for, there is no trade-off between inflation and unemployment because it is vertical and equal to the natural rate of unemployment.

Price—the sum of money necessary to purchase a good or service.

Price = MC—in a purely competitive market model, the principle that a firm's demand is perfectly elastic and equal to price, so that a firm will maximize profit when price equals marginal cost if price is equal to or greater than average total cost (ATC) and minimize loss if price is greater than average variable cost (AVC).

Price ceiling—a price set below equilibrium by government.

Price elasticity of demand—percentage of change in quantity demanded divided by percentage of change in price; measures responsiveness to price changes.

Price elasticity of supply—percentage of change in quantity supplied divided by percentage of change in price; measures responsiveness to price changes.

Price fixing—illegal collusion between producers to set an above-equilibrium price.

Price floor—a price set above equilibrium by government.

Producer surplus—that portion of the supply curve that lies below equilibrium price and denotes producers that would bring the goods or services to market at even lower prices.

Progressive tax—a marginal tax rate system in which the percentage of tax increases as income increases and vice versa (such as U.S. federal income tax brackets).

Proportional tax—a flat tax system in which the percentage of tax remains fixed as income changes.

Pure competition—market structure in which so many firms produce a very similar good or service that no firm has significant control over market price; a "price taker."

Pure monopoly—market structure in which one firm is the sole producer of a distinct good or service and thus has significant control over market price; a "price maker."

Quantity demanded—various amounts along a consumer demand curve showing the quantity consumers will buy at various prices.

Quantity supplied—various amounts along a producer supply curve showing the quantity producers will sell at various prices.

Recession—two consecutive business quarters of negative real gross domestic product (GDP).

Regressive tax—a set tax percentage the average rate of which decreases as the taxpayer's income increases, and vice versa; an example is sales tax.

Shortage—difference between the quantity demanded of a good or service and the quantity supplied at a below-equilibrium price ($Q_d > Q_s$).

Short run—the length of time during which a producer is unable to alter all the inputs of production.

Sole proprietorship—an unincorporated business owned by an individual.

Specialization—concentration of resource(s) in the production of a good or service that results in increased efficiency of production.

Stock—an ownership share in a company held by an investor.

Structural unemployment—unemployment resulting from a mismatch of worker skill to demand or location.

Substitute—goods or services that are interchangeable. When the price of one increases, the demand for the other increases.

Supply-side economics—macroeconomic perspective that emphasizes fiscal policies aimed at altering the state of the economy through I_g (short run) and the aggregate supply (long run).

Surplus—difference between the quantity demanded of a good or service and the quantity supplied at an above-equilibrium price ($Q_d < Q_s$).

Tariff—a tax on imports/exports.

Tax—a required payment of money to government, for which the payer receives no direct goods or services.

Trade deficit—amount by which a nation's imports exceed its exports.

Trade-off—forgone alternative use of a resource in the production of a good or service.

Trade surplus—amount by which a nation's exports exceed its imports.

Variable cost—cost of inputs that fluctuates as a firm increases or decreases its output.

Notes

Notes

Notes